Julia Bradbury is a well-loved television presenter, author, nature advocate and charity campaigner.

She is best known for turning her lifelong passion for walking into prime-time TV, with shows including *Britain's Best Walks*, *Cornwall and Devon Walks with Julia Bradbury* and *Wainwright's Walks in the Lake District*. She started her television career as a show business reporter for breakfast television in Los Angeles, coming home to help launch Channel 5 in the UK.

She was a key member of the presenting team that made *Countryfile* into one of the most watched factual programmes on BBC1, with millions tuning in on Sunday nights, and has fronted other flagship shows including *Top Gear* and *Watchdog*. In recent years she has also taken on a creative role, co-developing new series, as well as appearing on screen.

Julia's family has connections with Ireland, Rutland and Greece. She was born in Dublin and grew up in Sheffield, which is where she was introduced to walking and the power of the great outdoors by her father Michael. He would take her roaming across the Peak District, igniting a passion that remains to this day.

Julia is also a prolific writer with several books about walking, nature and travel to her name. This is her debut as a health and wellness author.

She has used her platform as a public figure to raise awareness and funds for organisations including the National Trust and Keep Britain Tidy and also served a ten-year term as the president of the Camping and Caravanning Club. Along with her sister Gina, Julia founded The Outdoor Guide website and foundation to encourage us all to get outdoors and enjoy green spaces – and hopefully to protect them, too.

Julia was awarded an honorary doctorate for 'outstanding merit' in her work by Sheffield Hallam University in 2013.

Following her 2021 diagnosis of breast cancer and her recovery from a mastectomy, she made an award-winning documentary, *Julia Bradbury: Breast Cancer & Me* about her experience and has become a champion for Britain's breast cancer charities. She has supported prostate, ovarian and bowel cancer charities for many years and also campaigns for better diagnosis, research and funding into the disease endometriosis.

Having discovered that around forty per cent of cancers are preventable, Julia is now determined to speak up for a more personalised approach to healthcare, embracing new science and taking a preventative and integrative approach.

Walk Yourself Happy distils what she's learned and reveals how we can all adopt happier, healthier lifestyles in the twenty-first century, using nature as our guide. The compelling evidence for better sleep, nutrition, breathing and exercise is explored, along with practical health hacks that we can all adopt, for free.

Julia lives in London with her long-term partner and is the mother of three children – a son and twin daughters. She takes them camping to stargaze and ensures they get regular doses of green therapy and nature – vitamin N. She can often be seen hugging trees and walking barefoot in the grass.

JULIA BRADBURY

WALK YOURSELF HAPPY

Find your path to
health and healing in nature

PIATKUS

PIATKUS

First published in Great Britain in 2023 by Piatkus

3 5 7 9 10 8 6 4

A CIP catalogue record for this book
is available from the British Library.

ISBN: 978-0-349-43623-4

Typeset in Adobe Garamond by Hewer Text UK Ltd, Edinburgh
Illustration on page 251 by Matt Baker; all other illustrations by Louise Turpin
Printed and bound in Great Britain by Clays Ltd, Elcograf S.p.A.

Papers used by Piatkus are from well-managed forests and other responsible sources.

Piatkus
An imprint of
Little, Brown Book Group
Carmelite House
50 Victoria Embankment
London EC4Y 0DZ

An Hachette UK Company
www.hachette.co.uk

www.littlebrown.co.uk

This book is dedicated to Team ZXZ.
I love you more than the universe itself.

Contents

Introduction

My name is Julia and I am an addict.

I'm addicted to the natural world. I love looking upwards through a canopy of trees to catch a glimpse of sky, tuning out life's noisy noise so my ears and head vibrate with birdsong instead, all while inhaling great clouds of fresh air through my nose.

Watching the surge of a full-moon tide thrills me as much as tracing my fingers around the helix of a fallen pine cone on a forest floor. I can't think of a better smell than the musky odour of earth after rain: the scent of life itself, geosmin.

The BBC current affairs programme *Newsnight* describes me as 'the outdoor evangelist Julia Bradbury', and I guess that's true. I'll take the compliment.

But it's only half the story. I don't just admire and enjoy nature; my real obsession is walking in it, using its healing powers to strengthen my body and soothe my mind. Walking is one of the simplest and best forms of physical exercise there is – but it is *so* much more than that.

Solvitur ambulando – literally, 'it is solved by walking' – is an idea that has been with us for a long time. St Augustine was preaching about it in the fourth century. Hundreds of years earlier, in 355 BCE, Aristotle founded the Peripatetic School in Athens, delivering philosophy lectures on the move. The nineteenth-century naturalists Henry David Thoreau and Charles Darwin were passionate advocates of walking and thinking, as were philosophers Søren Kierkegaard and Friedrich Nietzsche.

I believe there's a lesson for us all in that as we rise to the challenges of the twenty-first century. In this book, I'm going to give you practical advice on how to build walking and nature into your everyday life, and I'll explain how seemingly small additions and new habits can have a profound impact on your physical health and emotional well-being.

I'm not a doctor. Well, technically I *am* Dr Bradbury; I have an honorary doctorate from Sheffield Hallam University for outstanding merit in my work preserving natural landscapes and helping people appreciate them. What I mean is, I'm not a scientist – though in the coming chapters, I'll be talking to plenty of them. These are people at the forefront of the global quest to understand health and wellness. In Chapter 3, which is about nutrition, Professor Tim Spector tells us all about the gut microbiome and why 'gut instinct' really matters. This emerging science suggests that a healthy gut is one of the foundations of good health, impacting on everything from our immune systems to our moods. In Chapter 4, I talk to Professor Russell Foster who explains why sleep is so fundamentally important, how we repair ourselves at night and why prioritising sleep could lengthen our lives. Where does nature fit in to these two chapters you might be thinking? Well, we need healthy soils and rich biodiversity for every mouthful of food we eat and drop of water we drink. As for sleep, our body clocks should be in tune with natural daylight and darkness to optimise our wake/sleep cycle and in turn protect our health.

I might not be an academic like Professor Spector and Professor Foster but I do have decades of lived experience of walking as a curative. I've used it to help me through breast cancer and other physical traumas, as well as IVF and miscarriages, grief, mental health issues, and even a broken heart.

During my thirty years of making television shows and writing books, walking has taken me to the furthest corners of the world, introducing me to fascinating people and teaching me about cultures very different from my own.

I've trekked along the seaboard of the Indonesian archipelago, through the rainforests of Australia, across the Mongolian desert and over the South African veld. My roots are in Greece, and I've walked across a lot of the Greek islands too, digging into my Mama Mou Chrissi's family history. (By the way, the Greek word *peripatetikos*, which means 'of walking', gives us the English 'peripatetic'.)

What these very different expeditions had in common was their ability to heal my body, calm my mind and lift my heart. Together, they have helped me formulate my own theories on physical and mental health, finding happiness and being resilient in today's world.

You don't need big landscapes or seat-of-the-pants travel adventures to benefit from this kind of 'green therapy'; it can be found in short periods of time and the smallest of spaces. I call these moments 'nature snacks': fleeting moments in the natural world that can revive and nourish.

To explore this further, I have teamed up with Sue Stuart-Smith, renowned psychotherapist and author of the best-selling book *The Well-Gardened Mind*, which analyses the relationship between gardening and mental health. She acts as our resident therapist throughout *Walk Yourself Happy*, providing exercises and insights designed to help us form better psychological and emotional connections to nature.

In the wake of my 2021 cancer diagnosis, a simple daily walk to my local park gave me courage in the fight of my life. After my mastectomy, I used footsteps as a measure of my recovery. Short, tentative walks around my city garden gave me faith and brought me back to myself.

However, this is not a book about cancer. It is about walking yourself happy and healthy, wherever you find yourself in life, and whatever your situation.

There are inspiring stories from other people who have over-come serious life challenges of their own. You will be uplifted to hear about Louise, a grandmother who went from walking twenty-five steps a day and battling a dependence on prescription painkillers to walking 12,000 steps a day and rediscovering the joys of hiking and sea swimming. You will read about a young actress called Maude who turned her back on superstardom for the sake of her health. She'd starred in a globally successful TV drama, but left show business to seek joy and fulfilment as a meditation guide. Then there's broadcaster Mike Parry, who got off his hospital bed and walked away from a heart transplant operation – and has been walking ever since.

The thing about walking is that you don't need fancy kit or lots of money, a check sheet or a team leader. You don't need a high level of physical fitness or talent. Ego and ambition can be left at home. As for self-belief? That's what you're walking towards. To get started, you just lace up your shoes and put one foot in front of the other.

I have dedicated an entire chapter, Chapter 8, to explaining how to get going and keep going. With the help of green exercise expert Hannah Beadle, I guide you through the physical benefits of walking and outline the growing evidence that it can help stave off multiple diseases. In the hope you'll find it a gateway drug to doing even more exercise, Hannah and I have created a complete outdoor programme for muscle strength and mobility especially for this book.

While you are outside walking, and hopefully doing our exercises, don't forget to breathe – or rather, don't forget to breathe properly. In Chapter 5, world-famous breathing expert and author Patrick McKeown tells us how to take a real – and a metaphorical – healing breath every day. If you're anything like me, you probably breathe too much and not very efficiently, gulping in air, thinking you're doing a good job. Actually, you're not getting as much oxygen into your body as you imagine, and that has a downstream impact on your health. This is why yogis have focused on breathwork for thousands of years.

Reading the chapter on breathwork is likely to be both soothing and terrifying. Patrick has created a breathing exercise for you to do while you're walking, and there is also a breath-holding test to help you gauge your overall health. (Be warned: one of the tables indicates that you are, er . . . dead.)

Walking is something you do in harmony with nature, and it brings an abundance of benefits, including better sleep, better gut health and better breathing, as I have explained. Chapter 2 will show how it also brings you to a deeper understanding of gratitude, awe and wonder. Here, I speak to British author and journalist Oliver Burkeman about how to make time for these vital emotions, and broadcaster Angela Scanlon about how they finally helped her achieve a work–life balance. Meditation, practising gratitude and finding the time and motivation to be still and quiet are things I've learned to do. They have had a genuinely positive impact on my life which is why I want to share them with you.

In summary, I'll be exploring multiple pillars of good health in this book, while talking to some fascinating people, and explaining how you can make these pillars part of your daily life, too. It's not daunting, because they come as part of the package when you just *walk*.

Wild things

Throughout this book, you'll be reading a lot about why we need nature in our lives, every day. It could be as simple as having a plant in your house and a bird feeder on your balcony . . . honestly, it doesn't matter how simple or small the connection, it's the principle that counts. Nature makes humans feel good.

You know how to engage with it because you were born with something called 'biophilia', which is the instinctive need to connect with other forms of life. Like the word 'peripatetic', 'biophilia' has its roots in Greek, with *bio* meaning 'life', and *philia* meaning 'friendship and affinity'.

It translates as 'love of life'.

The biologist Edward O. Wilson popularised the term in his 1984 book *Biophilia*, in which he explained how our attraction to nature is genetically predetermined. We appreciate flowers, for example, because they often signal the coming of fruit, a feast for early man. We love blossom today because there is an elemental part of us that still anticipates that pleasure.

Here's another example. Humans respond to fractals in nature. Fractals are those never-ending patterns found in the whorl of a cloud, the spiral of a seashell, the splayed tail of a peacock and in lightning, ammonites and ferns. Go open your fridge and you might find some in your veggie drawer – on a head of broccoli, for example.

Fractals are why I find myself transported when I'm looking at trees and notice the way the pattern of trunk and branch repeats itself all the way up to the tiniest of twigs scratching the sky.

Even though we don't understand why, the human eye processes fractals with fluency. They're aesthetically pleasing to us and have a measurable impact on reducing our stress levels. If you go back 45,000 years, to when our ancestors were making the first rock and cave art for pleasure, they were drawing fractals. Think about the fractals of the *Bellis perennis* – the common daisy – and you will see there's nothing common about it.

The problem is that modern life can be brutal, and its burdens are diminishing our biophilia, our sense of belonging in this natural world. Staring at blue screens for huge swathes of the day, being constantly interrupted by noises and notifications, rushing everywhere but not walking anywhere – we are far removed from how we used to live and how we have evolved. We're more sedentary and spend more time indoors than at any time in human history, and this is dangerous because we need our daily dose of vitamin N (Nature), especially in times of crisis. I do believe that the way we live now, with the twenty-four-hour-a-day demands of work and family life, constitutes a crisis, even if we don't always call it that.

More than a century ago, as World War One raged, British and German soldiers sought solace from birds in the hedgerows and hares in the fields; they adopted pet ducks, tamed feral cats, improvised fishing trips and grew vegetables in tiny gardens at the ends of their trenches. They practised botany on the front line.

We can learn a lot from that instinctive response, their embracing of nature in a time of threat.

How we live now

'Biophilia' was a plea for mankind to be ethical, to conserve wild and beautiful places, and to protect the world's animals in all their diversity. Edward O. Wilson wanted to tell us that without a robust natural world, we humans can't prosper. Yes, we need economic security, but we also need clean air, healthy soil, plenty of trees and the vast array of environments Earth has to offer: its deserts, forests, oceans, mountains and icecaps.

I do hope we are waking up to the need to take care of our world, ourselves and each other. The brilliant thing about walking is that it can help you do all three at the same time.

It's the best form of everyday travel for humans because it creates oneness with nature, camaraderie with friends and a form of intimacy with oneself. It can calm the mind or inspire big dreams; it can invigorate the body and ensure we live better, for longer. We are bipeds for a reason.

So, come with me as I lead the way on the walk of our lifetimes, one where we can walk ourselves happy, one sublime step at a time.

1

The Mistress of Worry . . . Anxiety

'Now is the age of anxiety.'
W. H. Auden, *The Age of Anxiety*

When the poet W. H. Auden died in 1973, half a century before I wrote this, his obituary in the *New York Times* said his 'singular voice gave resonance to a troubled age'.

Anxiety is not new, although it is perhaps more prevalent today as we find ourselves buffeted by twenty-first-century life.

We are hurried, harried, hyperconnected and, more often than we'd like, heartsore. Sometimes we can feel helpless and, at our bleakest, hopeless. Anxiety exists across all genders, age groups and sections of society. It is challenging even for those with the kind of power, wealth and fame that would once have been thought to inoculate against it.

Full disclosure: I'm not a particularly anxious person. I don't get anxious walking into a roomful of strangers, I've never had a panic attack and I don't have any triggers. That doesn't mean I've never felt anxious or that I'm always the confident woman you see onscreen.

Anxiety is a universal experience, and I've certainly lived through times where I have felt sick with worry or sadness. On occasions, I've felt anxious and 'shy' about doing something perfectly normal, like greeting a neighbour on the street (despite not feeling flustered while broadcasting a live show to millions of people). During the first lockdown of the Covid pandemic, I had an inexplicably furious encounter with the iron, which led to two hours of crying. Was that a mini-breakdown, a bout of pandemic-related anxiety about what it meant for our lives? I'm still not sure.

At work, I can look back on anxious times, like the time I became entangled in a tabloid story that nearly ruined my career, or when I had a damaging internal dispute with a boss who had control over my professional future. In private, I faced a personally devastating diagnosis of endometriosis in my thirties, jeopardising my chances of becoming a mother.

At the time, I perceived these as challenging life events but now, knowing what I do, I can see they were much more than that and I was suffering bouts of anxiety throughout each of them. So what did I do? Well, on one occasion I packed a rucksack for a once-in-a-lifetime expedition to Iceland's volcanic uplands at a time when I was praying I was pregnant. It was another example of my failure to nail my work–life balance – the thing that brings us all true harmony. Without acknowledging it, this was one of the greatest sources of anxiety that I have ever known.

I will tell you about those difficult days – and how I coped – a little later.

What is anxiety?

We will all face distressing, anxiety-inducing times in our lives. Hopefully, none will embed themselves in our psyches and lead to a full-blown anxiety disorder, but it's sensible for us to understand what anxiety is, so we can recognise it in ourselves and others.

So, how do we define anxiety? Neuroscience tells us it's marked by excessive fear and avoidance, often in response to specific objects or situations. It could be experienced by a teenager turning over an exam paper, a forty-something divorcee starting to date again, or you asking for that pay rise you know you deserve.

The key thing is that it's a fear response in the absence of true danger.

Sue Stuart-Smith is the resident psychotherapist who's here to help me with *Walk Yourself Happy*. She shares my belief in the healing power of nature. She is married to the garden designer Tom Stuart-Smith, and their shared life's work can be seen in the Barn Gardens in Serge Hill, Hertfordshire, where they have lived since the 1980s. Tom was actually born in Serge Hill, which has been in his family for a century.

Deep roots, indeed.

I asked her for her expert definition of anxiety. Sue tells us:

Anxiety is a normal response to stress. Most of us will feel anxious and worried in the face of threatening or stressful situations, and in many instances, it would be a serious disadvantage not to. In evolutionary terms, anxiety is a survival tool because it acts like a signal, prompting us to act in the face of danger. This is our fight-or-flight response, which is coordinated by the amygdala, the fear centre located deep within the brain.

The fight-or-flight response involves activation of our sympathetic nervous system with immediate release of adrenaline, which prepares us to react by raising our heart rate and blood pressure, releasing glucose and speeding up our breathing. Following on from this, if the threat persists, the stress hormone cortisol is released. In most circumstances, once danger has passed, our bodies recover through the restorative effects of the parasympathetic, or rest-and-digest, system.

Problems arise when our fear response is either disproportionate or prolonged, so there is no recovery time. When we are unable to relax or 'switch off', anxiety easily becomes a vicious circle. The more anxious we feel, the more we overthink situations and envisage worst-case scenarios. This, in turn, feeds anxiety and is exhausting. When the mind is overactive and full of trepidation like this, we inevitably find it hard to focus and function productively. When this happens, our threshold for coping with life can diminish to such an extent that everyday hassles we would normally cope with can start to feel like insurmountable obstacles.

Apart from the hallmark feelings of dread and worry, anxiety can manifest itself in different ways. Some people find themselves becoming unusually irritable, others feel low and tearful. Some feel too nauseous to eat, while others take refuge in the comfort of food. At night, it can be hard to switch off and difficulties getting to sleep and staying asleep are common. But insomnia is not always a problem; some people find themselves sleeping excessively, yet find on waking that they feel unrefreshed.

The effects of anxiety can be experienced mainly in the body or mainly in the mind, or a mixture of the two. Panic attacks, for example, are a bodily manifestation of anxiety that typically seem to come out of nowhere. A pounding heartbeat is accompanied by trembling, sweating and sometimes fainting, alongside a feeling of doom. Attacks like this inevitably lead to a fear of them happening again, and they are so unpleasant that most people feel compelled to avoid situations in which they've occurred. By contrast, generalised anxiety is characterised by ever-present and uncontrollable worries about many different aspects of life.

Other forms of anxiety, such as phobias, are more specific and triggered by certain situations, such as encountering spiders or experiencing heights. Some phobias have profoundly restrictive effects on everyday life. Agoraphobia involves a fear of unfamiliar settings and typically leads to avoidance of public transport and crowded as well as open spaces. Social anxiety, likewise, can cause isolation, because an intense fear of being ridiculed or rejected leads to an avoidance of social situations.

To some extent, depression and anxiety go hand in hand, and although they are distinct, they frequently occur together. Whatever the type of anxiety someone is suffering from, if it is interfering with everyday life, it is important to seek help.

A pandemic of anxiety

You might have thought the Covid pandemic would have seriously impacted our anxiety levels, but there's increasing evidence that it didn't do quite as much damage as initially suggested (although we are of course yet to know the true long-term consequences). A review of 137 separate studies from around the world, carried out by researchers at McGill University in Canada and published in the *British Medical Journal*, said many doom-laden predictions of a spike in anxiety cases and small-scale investigations simply went around the world on repeat.

The real issue is not Covid – it's twenty-first-century life.

According to the charity Anxiety UK, twenty-one per cent of us were already suffering 'high' anxiety levels in 2019, a year before Covid hit. And it's not just the UK; in the United States, according to a recent epidemiological study, the lifetime prevalence of any anxiety disorder is 28.8 per cent.[1]

As a partner, colleague, friend and family member, it's on my radar. And, as the mother of three young children, I'm also particularly concerned about the exponential rise of teen anxiety. I don't have all the answers, but I do know that nature soothes and heals, and that being in it banks a goodness and strength we can draw on when we need to.

A walk in nature walks the soul back home

As I said earlier, anxiety has wrong-footed me. Unsurprisingly, for someone who grew up wanting to recreate their happy childhood with a family of their own, it came at a time I was struggling with infertility.

I had been commissioned to do one of the walks of my lifetime, through the volcanic highlands of Iceland, along the sixty-kilometre Landmannalaugar trail. I've been walking since I was a little girl, in the Lakes, the Peak District, along the Cornish cliffs and over the South Downs, in Scotland and Wales, and across the flatlands of the Norfolk coast.

Iceland, however, was in another league; this would be a trek through the fire and ice of a mythologised landscape. Professionally, it was significant too. It was a pivotal moment in my career; I was making a documentary that was a shift in direction away from the Sunday-night prime-time series that had made my name.

But it wasn't this gamble with the Bradbury brand, or the industry eyes scrutinising it, that was making me anxious. What was making me feel sick and scared was a pregnancy test, bought at a pharmacy in London and tucked into a secret pocket of my enormous backpack.

I had previously undergone keyhole surgery for the endometriosis that had stopped me getting pregnant. This was the month I hoped I might finally have a baby on the way. Of course, I could not tell my crew that, on the day I would be striding towards a famous volcano on camera, I was going to have to stop to pee on a pregnancy test. Nor could I share the moment with my partner, who, while he would never say 'Julia, don't go!' was at home, privately wishing I had a desk job.

If you are wondering whether you are pregnant and Option A is to put your feet up and have a cuppa, while Option B is to go on an expedition involving cliff edges, icy rapid crossings and helicopters, then the risk assessment is always going to say: Don't do Option B.

Too late. I was already up a volcano.

Today, the more I know about anxiety, the more I wonder if taking this all-consuming challenge was a way of avoiding the fact that I might not be able to get pregnant at all?

Then aged thirty-eight, I was desperate for motherhood, but I had to balance my baby hunger against a job I loved, and that would sustain me no matter what. That's why I found myself trying to have both, and doing a pregnancy test in an isolated shepherd's hut. I hid in the long-drop toilet, partly exposed to the elements, and waited for two minutes.

They felt like the longest 120 seconds of my life.

Sadly, the blue line stayed stubbornly single. There was no second line indicating a positive test. I wasn't pregnant. There was no baby.

I could feel anxiety seeding inside me. Was I ever going to fall pregnant? Would my body, with all that I asked of it, be allowed to do this most natural of things? Was childlessness the price I had to pay for pursuing my passion projects?

I should say here I understand and respect anyone's decision to be child-free. But that wasn't me. We dearly wanted to be parents, and this was devastating.

The drama of the scenery reflected the turmoil inside me. I could not sit still or calm my heart, even with deep breathing. My body was burning with an anxious energy I could barely contain.

If you'd asked me what I wanted at that precise moment, I'd have said, 'An exorcism.'

I'd known I would have to take the test and where, and I had also known, in theory, that it might be negative. However, the fact of it, in my hand, brought the balance of my life – and my future – into the sharpest focus. With my camera crew waiting and a shooting schedule to keep, I had no choice but to step out into the crisp Icelandic morning.

What followed was the perfect example of how landscapes can reset our personal view of ourselves. I let myself see that I was part of a huge vista of mountains, icy streams, steaming hillsides and bubbling, sulphurous mud pools. I acknowledged that even this grandeur was just a tiny part of our universe and that I was no more than a speck within it. Against the vastness and beauty of that idea, my problems seemed smaller, less complicated, more manageable.

It felt like the end of an intense few months, but it did not feel like the end of hope.

Over the hours that followed, in the natural craziness of those icy uplands, I hiked my heart out. I knew that, if I allowed it, nature would heal me. I'd let the sheer physicality of the next twenty kilometres exhaust me, devoting those hours of climbing, scrambling and slipping to processing what had just happened.

Inside, desolation gave way at first to a sense of perspective and then to a warming positivity. I was only midway through my walk, my big adventure, my big deal. That meant, surely, the best was yet to come.

It was a metaphor for the rest of my life.

By the close of that day, when I crawled, exhausted, into my sleeping bag, I felt a lightness that had been missing for months. In walking, I was reminded of all the things my body could do; the toughness of the terrain reaffirmed my body's capability and its strength. The enormity of the space allowed me to feel that I was just travelling through, not at my journey's end.

I could go home, trusting myself to try again.

I would go on to have my son naturally. One miscarriage and four rounds of IVF treatment later, my twin daughters arrived.

I've been a mother for more than a decade now, but anxiety still makes an unwelcome appearance in my life from time to time – something that comes as no surprise to Sue. I asked her why anxiety is so prevalent now.

We live in an age of anxiety and there is, in truth, a lot to be anxious about. A long period of austerity, coupled with the economic and social aftermath of the pandemic, has created a sense of the precariousness of life. At the same time, global situations such as the war in Ukraine and climate change also weigh heavily on us. These are all situations that can leave us feeling powerless and insecure.

Over the last decade or so, studies show that anxiety has undoubtedly been on the rise. A large increase was recorded following the financial crash of 2008, and levels have remained high ever since, particularly among women and young people. Anxiety is the most commonly experienced of all the mental health disorders, with one in four people suffering from it at some point in their lives.[2]

Some of this rise may be because people feel more able to acknowledge their struggle with mental health, but there are also social and lifestyle factors that are playing a part. These include rising levels of loneliness and financial insecurity, coupled with a culture of overwork.

Social media is often blamed for its damaging effects on self-esteem and for the compulsive habits it encourages, detracting from other, healthier aspects of life. Digital technology in general makes it hard for us to 'switch off', and as a result, the differentiation between work time and downtime, daytime and night-time has been lost. This leads to a disruption of our basic biological rhythms and makes it harder to recover from stress.

We are embedded in a culture of speed in which, for the most part, the quicker things happen, the better. This unremitting pace of life has led to a devaluing of the slower rhythms of natural time, and in various ways we are encouraged to defy our biological limits. One of the reasons walking can be so helpful for us is that travelling by foot simply forces us to slow down.

Air apparent

How can we heal ourselves, quell those anxious feelings and make space for the happiness and equilibrium we deserve? I achieved it in Iceland, but there's more to it than just a pretty view. It's about the science of fresh air and daylight, and the immersion of our senses of touch, taste, sight, smell and hearing.

As Sue says in her book *The Well-Gardened Mind*, Florence Nightingale was on to something way back in the nineteenth century. In her *Notes on Nursing*, published in 1859, the nursing pioneer underlined the importance of fresh air: 'Always air from the air without, and that, too, through those windows through which the air comes freshest.'

Nightingale also noticed that patients recovered faster when attention was paid to their surroundings. 'People say the effect [of their surroundings] is only on the mind. It is no such thing. The effect is on the body, too. Little as we do know about the way in which we are affected by form, colour and light, we do know this, that they have an actual physical effect.' (Even today we're still not completely sure how this works but the emerging science of quantum biology may soon provide us with answers. In a nutshell it means we might one day be able to control physiological processes by using the quantum properties of biological matter.)

Yet natural light, our environment and fresh air were all officially identified back in the 1800s as vital to human health – and, more significantly, as helpful tools in our recovery from illness, both mental and physical.

Robin's story: The power of flowers

Robin Hanbury-Tenison was eighty-four when he contracted coronavirus in 2020 and was given a five per cent chance of survival. 'I went down badly with Covid in March, and my family was told to expect the worst. I was in intensive care for five weeks and in hospital for seven. I should have died, at my age. But the wonderful doctors pulled me through,' he says.

It was a remarkable and unexpected turnaround, but Robin puts his recovery down to nature (as well as his doctors). He said the moment he knew he was going to live was when he was wheeled into the healing garden at Derriford Hospital in Plymouth. 'I opened my eyes, saw the sunshine, the flowers, and that was when I was certain my life had been saved by the healing power of nature. From then on, everything picked up.'

Robin is an extraordinary man, and that shouldn't be discounted from his story. A renowned explorer, he made a landmark crossing of South America at its widest point in 1958, and led a Royal Geographical Society expedition to Borneo in 1977, which was dedicated to the preservation of the Mulu rainforest. He's campaigned for decades to safeguard the Amazon and the rights of indigenous and tribal peoples through Survival International, which he co-founded.

Clearly, he's someone who's been connected to nature all his life – and when he needed it, nature saved him.

Robin was so grateful for his second chance that he set up a GoFundMe page because, in his opinion, 'every hospital in Britain should have a healing garden attached to the intensive care unit'.

After he was discharged, Robin could barely walk five yards with a Zimmer frame, but he set himself the challenge of climbing Cornwall's highest peak, Brown Willy, to kick-start the fund. Five months after he crawled out of hospital, and with Storm Alex blowing, he planted a Cornish flag on the summit, 420 metres above sea level.

That's the healing power of nature right there: Robin's flag marked the spot. (He has since raised more than £150,000 and funded a hospital healing garden in his home county of Cornwall.)

Darkness cannot drive out darkness: only the light can do that

There is no doubt in my mind that being surrounded by the glories of nature in Iceland helped me deal with my infertility, but there was something else at play, too: daylight and sunshine.

We know that daylight is an essential component of our overall health, and it's instrumental in altering our mood. For many, like me (I'm half Greek) it's a source of happiness and well-being.

The science of the sun has long been understood by humans. The Babylonian king Hammurabi advised priests to use sunlight in the treatment of illness almost 4,000 years ago. Ancient Egyptians worshipped Ra, a falcon-headed god who carried the sun disc on his headdress. Greek physicians who worked with Hippocrates recommended it for the restoration of health, and we know what Florence Nightingale's thoughts were on the subject.

You won't find a cameraperson or photographer who doesn't want to film or take pictures in Iceland, because the light there is so magical. Its location in the North Atlantic, between Greenland and Norway, just south of the Arctic Circle, means it has some of the most beautiful and unusual light patterns in the world. And there I was, bathing in that loveliness for six days straight.

In her book *Chasing the Sun: The New Science of Sunlight and How it Shapes our Bodies and Minds*, the award-winning science journalist Linda Geddes writes about the circadian rhythms that govern our bodies, explaining that these internal body clocks are regulated by light. Whether they are instructing our immune cells in their fight against disease, or dictating our response to food, or telling our bodies when to be alert and when to rest, our master clock is keeping time with daylight, so exposure to the daily light–dark cycle is one of the most fundamental things we can do to support our health.

When your circadian rhythm is disrupted, it can contribute to a variety of chronic health conditions: sleep disorders, obesity, type 2 diabetes, depression, bipolar disorder and seasonal affective disorder (SAD). Light affects the production of the sleep-promoting hormone melatonin, too.

Surrounding light – the outside light that envelops you – is always better than artificial light, because it's stronger and brighter (though don't forget your big hat and long sleeves!). Sunlight typically registers anywhere between 50,000 and 100,000 lux (the unit used to measure light). This is way higher than your average lightbulb, which is 250–500 lux. It's only in very recent decades that we humans have become an 'indoor society', with many of us now spending ninety per cent of our day indoors under artificial light, which has even become known as an 'indoor epidemic'. Don't you notice how tired and drained you feel after a day spent under this type of lighting? I know I do. Getting outside, even on a dull day, is important.

Sunlight, darkness and artificial light all determine your cortisol levels, too. Cortisol, which we'll talk about again and again in this book, is the body's main stress hormone. Too much isn't good, and neither is too little. If you aren't getting enough daylight, or if you are exposing your eyes and skin to artificial light at night, when your body needs darkness, you may be throwing off your natural balance.

This means trouble because, along with playing an important role in your circadian rhythms, cortisol can also help control blood sugar levels, regulate the metabolism, reduce inflammation, and assist with memory formulation.[3] It has a controlling effect on salt and water balance, and helps control blood pressure.

So, quite important then.

Stress raises our cortisol levels, and I'm guessing mine would have been off the scale if not for that Icelandic light and the natural rhythms of days spent getting up with the sun and turning in when darkness fell.

At the same time, the northern sunshine would have been upping my levels of vitamin D – low levels of which are linked to depression and anxiety. The sun is our primary source of 'the sunshine vitamin', and, according to the World Health

Organization (WHO), just five to fifteen minutes of sunlight on your arms, hands and face two or three times a week is enough to reap its benefits.[4]

In summary, I was getting a generous dose of sunshine and natural daylight while walking away my pain. The landscape was inspiring in me a sense of gratitude, awe and wonder, reminding me at every turn that I was part of the world wide web of nature.

It was the perfect prescription. I was right where I needed to be.

Ice baby

In Iceland, and other Nordic countries including Denmark and Sweden, it is common to see babies left in prams in open gardens or on porches, sleeping in the fresh air. You also see babies snoozing outside cafés and restaurants. (The crime rate in Iceland is incredibly low, particularly violent crime – though let's not talk about financial crime.)

The tradition originates from when Icelanders lived in turf houses. Mainly buried beneath the earth, the interiors were really unpleasant: dirty, over-stuffed with people and animals, and with terrible ventilation.

Keeping your baby outside was beneficial for their health in those days, and the custom has stuck. Today, Iceland is one of the healthiest countries in the world, with an extremely long life expectancy and low rates of infant mortality.

120 minutes of nature

I was fortunate enough to be in Iceland when I needed my nature cure, but you can seek it out *anywhere*.

A study published by the University of Exeter reveals that 120 minutes a week spent in green spaces has a beneficial impact on your life.[5] You don't even need to enjoy those minutes consecutively; you just need to spend a minimum of two hours a week outside to reap the rewards of vitamin N (nature) and vitamin D (daylight). And what better way to spend those two hours than walking? Vitamin Sea helps, too, if you are anywhere near the coast!

Thanks to the work of Dr Qing Li, an immunologist and forest medicine expert, we also understand more about the benefits of forest bathing, the name given to spending time among trees. In his 2018 book, *Into the Forest*, Dr Li shows that the physiological benefits of three hours of forest bathing remain in the body for a fortnight or more.

I asked Sue, *Walk Yourself Happy*'s resident psychotherapist, why – and how – nature works.

One of the best descriptions I have come across of the effects of the natural world on us was written in the nineteenth century by the American landscape designer and creator of New York's Central Park, Frederick Law Olmsted.

He was a pioneer of the public park and believed it was vital for people to have access to beautiful green spaces within cities in order to improve their health. Spending time in nature, he wrote: 'employs the mind without fatigue and yet exercises it; tranquilises it and yet enlivens it; and thus, through the influence of the mind over the body, gives the effect of refreshing rest and reinvigoration to the whole system'.

The science to back up Olmsted's observations didn't exist back then, but there are now hundreds of studies that prove him right. Healthy changes in heart rate and blood pressure can be detected within a few minutes of being in nature, while levels of the stress hormone cortisol typically start to drop after thirty minutes. Other studies have shown reductions in anxiety and improvements in mood. Even gazing at a view of trees through a window can help restore mental energy and benefit our powers of attention. Studies that have compared the effects of walking in a park with walking along a highway have found that those who walked in nature dwelt less on anxious or negative thoughts and performed better in subsequent cognitive tests.

Of course, all forms of exercise are beneficial for us. The physical benefits get the most attention, but exercise has important effects on the brain through the release of mood-boosting neurotransmitters, such as endorphins, dopamine and serotonin, and also through raising levels of brain-derived neurotrophic factor (BDNF), which keeps the brain healthy. While most forms of exercise will reduce stress, the more we are immersed in an activity and the more we enjoy it, the more effective it is.

There is now a substantial body of research that shows that 'green exercise', as it's come to be known, is more beneficial for us than working out in a gym. Some of this effect is down to exposure to greenery, fresh air and sunlight, but some is simply down to pure pleasure.

Increasing numbers of GPs are issuing 'social prescriptions' for green activities, such as walking, nature conservation and gardening, to help a range of conditions including heart disease, hypertension, diabetes, stress, depression and anxiety. When the UK Wildlife Trusts conducted a cost-benefit analysis on the nature-based programmes they ran in 2019, they found that for every £1 invested, there was a £6.88 return in terms of increased well-being.[6]

The fact that spending time in nature can have such far-reaching beneficial effects on us should not be surprising, for we are, in origin, a grassland species. Landscapes containing flowering plants, trees and greenery were conducive to our hunter-gatherer ancestors' survival. You could say that experiencing a connection to nature fulfils a deep ancestral need. Certainly, our bodies are best adapted to nature. Over the course of human evolution, our nervous systems and immune systems have been primed to respond to key aspects of the natural world.

For example, the brain is much more efficient at processing the visual patterns found in nature than those we commonly encounter in cities. Natural surroundings are conducive to 'fluent visual processing' – in other words, we are able to sweep over the environment with a relaxed gaze, taking it in while making a minimum number of eye fixations. By contrast, built environments are characterised by harsh and irregular patterns, and research has shown that these require more eye fixations and therefore greater effort for the brain to collate the information.

The visual patterns we encounter in nature are typified by 'fractal patterning'. This involves repeated versions of the same patterns on different scales. One of the clearest examples of this is a tree that repeats its branching form throughout its entire structure in ways that are both regular and variable. Because fractal patterning contains an element of predictability, the visual cortex can fill in any gaps and effortlessly assemble a larger picture.

Much of the soundscape of nature is likewise gentle on the brain. Sounds such as the wind blowing through trees, gently flowing water and birdsong are restful because, like fractals, they are variable within a predictable range. The overall effect on our nervous system is, as Olmsted observed, one of relaxation and reinvigoration. In comparison, the noise of the city tends to be unpredictable and jarring, putting us on edge.

Finally, we cannot consider why nature is good for us without acknowledging the power of beauty. How often do we stop to admire a view, or gaze in wonder at the perfection of a flower? Brain-scan research shows that experiences of beauty like this are accompanied by neural activation of the deep emotional centres of the brain – regions that are associated with romantic love. These networks form part of our pleasure and reward pathways, and they play a vital role in integrating our thoughts, feelings and motivations, as well as damping down our fear and stress responses.

Introducing natural beauty through small gardens and parks in deprived urban areas has been found to reduce the incidence of crime as well as levels of depression and stress. Beautiful flowers and views of natural scenery can make a huge difference to how people cope with being in hospital. The benefits include needing less pain relief, experiencing less stress and anxiety, and, in some studies, being discharged more quickly.

Beauty is often regarded as a desirable but non-essential ingredient of life. But a need for it lies deep within us because beauty is a form of emotional nourishment. Sigmund Freud, who had a great passion for flowers, once commented that while beauty 'cannot protect us from suffering, it can compensate for a great deal'.

The Well-Gardened Mind with Sue Stuart-Smith

Early in World War One, in the spring of 1915, Sue's grandfather, Ted May, was taken prisoner of war in Turkey when the submarine he was serving on ran aground. He spent most of the rest of the war in a series of brutal labour camps where the death rates were high, and he was lucky to survive. Somehow, he managed to escape in 1918, and make the 4,000-mile journey back to England.

Sue picks up the story:

By the time he arrived home, Ted was severely malnourished as well as traumatised. My grandmother's loving and attentive care helped him regain some of his physical strength, but his traumas stayed with him, and in 1919 he was discharged from the naval service with a diagnosis of neurasthenia – a catch-all diagnosis of that era that indicated in everyday language a state of shattered nerves.

During the summer of 1920, he was given the chance to enrol on a rehabilitation programme in horticulture. What he experienced next was a form of nature cure, not of a magical kind, but of the kind that arises gradually through spending time in the refuge of a garden and being immersed in the natural world.

The garden that helped transform Ted's health belonged to a mansion called Sarisbury Court on the south coast of England. During the war, the largest American military hospital in Europe was located in its grounds. After the war, the British government developed it as a centre offering training courses for ex-servicemen who needed help to rebuild their lives.

The extensive and beautiful gardens that belonged to the mansion contained lakes with islands planted with tree ferns, and now form a public park called Holly Hill. There was also a large walled garden where Ted spent twelve months learning how to cultivate fruits and vegetables, as well as exotic plants, which grew in ten great glasshouses. His experience left him with a lifelong love of gardening – and in particular, a love of growing orchids.

Ted's eventual reconciliation to the appalling abuses he experienced, and his subsequent long and healthy life, are testament to the restorative effects of nature.

The Glasshouse effect

I wasn't surprised to learn this facet of Sue's family history, as I've been an advocate for a social enterprise called The Glasshouse for a number of years now. The mission, co-founded by project director Kali Hamerton-Stove and social entrepreneur Melissa Murdoch, aims to reduce reoffending through horticultural training and employment in UK prisons.

In The Glasshouse, ex-offenders grow and nurture beautiful houseplants, which are then sold in ethically sourced pots and baskets through their online shop.

The project, based at East Sutton Park, a women's prison in Kent, is built on 'the proven physical and emotional benefits that being close to nature provides'. It offers women the chance to earn a Level 2 horticulture qualification and then, on release, helps them find a job and a home. Many UK prisons have disused glass houses because of cuts in training and services, so the project also brings life to these unused physical resources.

I think it's brilliant on several levels. In addition to the obvious benefits for inmates while they're inside, many female prisoners have no skilled employment prospects and NFA – no fixed abode – when they're released. Giving them help to move forward with life after prison is invaluable – plus, the world needs more plants.

You can order some for your home or office via their website www.theglasshouse.co.uk and support this bold botanic initiative. What's more, as you'll see in Chapter 4, greenery is great for turning your bedroom into a sleep sanctuary.

Screen scream

Every generation of parents will say they are living in a time of unprecedented danger for their children. My own parents worried about television, that illuminated box in the corner of the room, fearing it would turn us young people into mindless zombies. Society, they thought, would crumble in the face of the cathode ray. We are in the age of the smartphone now, and the TV seems positively benign.

The human race has undergone a sophisticated digital revolution, but the result is us sitting down (bad), looking at screens (bad), not engaging with nature (bad), not talking to other people in real life (bad), and snacking on junk food (terrible). While our minds whirr, our bodies are more sedentary. Hard physical labour is no longer part of our everyday, and activities like walking to the shops or getting up from the sofa to switch

TV channels are becoming obsolete. Today more people suffer from obesity than starvation.

Also, mentally, we are always switched on. There is no such thing as 'off' when you have a phone in your pocket. Being able to see the rest of the world – and be seen by it – means we are constantly measuring ourselves against others, whether it's in terms of the width of our thigh gap, the contents of our fridge or our political opinions. There is no escape. We are hyperconnected, unless we choose to consciously switch ourselves off. When I interviewed Doctor Rory Conn, a leading child psychologist for the Radio 4 programme *One to One*, he described our children as the 'canaries down the coal mine' when it comes to the impact of this relentless exposure to social media and cyber space on their mental health.[7]

And we have a lot else besides our digital life to make us anxious. There's the ongoing shift to AI and the decline of traditional jobs and a secure workplace. We're trying to find love online instead of meeting a friend of a friend organically, as I did way back in the nineties. Families are more dislocated than ever before. We all have eco anxiety, and rightly so. Covid brought a new and terrifying health scare, a harsh economic legacy and the infringement of our liberty.

The W. H. Auden quote I shared at the start of the chapter about the age of anxiety comes around the time of World War Two – but it still resonates, doesn't it?

Helping yourself

It is important to use every tool we have available to help ourselves and each other. I walked in Iceland. Most of us, me included, can't usually do that. But we can seek a cure from nature by embracing green spaces, daylight and sunshine.

I can recommend:

Walking

Of course! Incorporating exercise into your daily routine is critical when it comes to keeping anxiety at bay. This has always been the way in cultures far older than ours. For example, practitioners of Aboriginal medicine believe the health of our bodies and minds are inextricably bound and that a person's 'spirit' can be healed partly by making their body well and strong.

Breathing

This is so important there's a whole chapter devoted to it later in the book. Intentional and slow breathing (that's six breaths a minute, compared to our normal ten to fourteen) is a simple way to stimulate the vagus nerve, the longest nerve in the body, which stretches from the brain through the body, via your stomach, intestines, heart and lungs. (*Vagus* means 'wanderer' in Latin, because it wanders all over.) This nerve is a part of our parasympathetic nervous system, which helps the body relax.

Food and drink

What you eat and drink plays such a significant part in your physical and mental health there's a whole chapter devoted to that, too. Odds are you know the basics already: reduce your caffeine intake and eliminate as much sugar as you can. Cut your alcohol consumption or stop drinking completely, and avoid recreational drug use. Drugs and alcohol may alleviate anxiety in the short term but they *will* exacerbate it over time.

Smells and essential oils

Part of the reason forest bathing is so good for you is that it lets you inhale the smells of trees and plants that are beneficial to human health and can reduce our stress levels. You can recreate those benefits in your own home. Some favourites include chamomile for sleep, orange for meditation, sandalwood for anxiety, clary sage and ylang ylang for stress and lemon to lift your mood. These have been trusted remedies for centuries. Note: only use therapeutic-grade oils, and don't ingest them. Seek advice if you're pregnant or breastfeeding, and be aware that some oils can be toxic to pets.

Sue suggests:

Because anxious thinking is focused on the future, anything that brings us back into the present moment is helpful. Mindfulness is very effective, but meditation exercises don't suit everyone. You can, in truth, carry out any activity mindfully – including walking and even doing the washing-up – simply by closely attending to your surroundings and your sensations. Certain activities require such a high level of focus that they have mindfulness built into them; many sports come into this category, as do crafting and making music. They're the kinds of activities that help you reset by transforming how you feel.

The most effective forms of treatment for anxiety are psychological, although medication may be needed if anxiety is severe. Cognitive behavioural therapy (CBT) is effective at alleviating panic attacks through relaxation and stress-reduction techniques. CBT can also help address negative cycles of thinking in more generalised forms of anxiety. Sometimes anxiety is a manifestation of unacknowledged feelings of grief or anger, and it is not uncommon for problems with anxiety to be triggered by life events involving a loss or trauma. In these situations, psychotherapy can provide a safe space in which to express and understand these experiences and the feelings associated with them.

Health screening, including thyroid function tests and vitamin D levels, is worth considering because various underlying disorders can contribute to high levels of anxiety. Many people with anxiety struggle on alone because they feel too anxious or ashamed to speak about it, but if your anxiety is interfering with everyday life, it's important to talk to your GP. Remember, the route to help is first through acknowledging that there is a problem.

The last word

As Matt Haig, whose books include *Notes on a Nervous Planet* and *Reasons to Stay Alive*, says, 'One frustration with anxiety is it is often hard to find a reason behind it. There may be no visible threat and yet you can feel utterly terrified. It's all intense suspense, no action. It's like *Jaws* without the shark.'[8] As I said at the start of this chapter, anxiety is a fear response in the absence of true danger. There really is no shark.

You don't have to be defeated or defined by anxious thoughts. You can soothe them, find quietness, and discover the joy and strength available to you every day, for free, in nature. No matter what challenges you face, I promise there is a walk that will inspire and right you. Walking has the dual power of being able to calm us and stimulate us when needed, as prescribed.

 Sue's seeds of wisdom: Walk it out

This exercise is inspired by a poem written by the great romantic writer Samuel Taylor Coleridge.

His poem 'This Lime-Tree Bower My Prison' is based on his own experience when an injury prevented him from walking in the hills he knew and loved with his friends. Left behind in a garden that he regards as a prison, he feels miserable and his mind dwells on the experiences he is missing. After a while, he finds himself entranced by the dappling of the sunlight on the leaves of the trees and starts listening to the sound of a nearby bee. No longer feeling himself imprisoned, his perception of the garden is transformed, as he realises how much beauty there is all around him.

If you don't have access to a garden, you can do this exercise in a park.

With each step you take, focus on the feeling of the ground beneath your feet and the air on your face. Tune in to the birds singing in the trees and the sound of wind rustling the leaves. After a while, you can stop and sit under a tree like Coleridge did, or lie on the grass and look at the world from a different perspective.

Then resume your walk and focus on your sense of smell. This is the most powerful and primitive of our senses, because recep-tors in the nose are in direct communication with the centres for emotion and memory deep within the brain.

Take time to stop and inhale the fragrance of any scented plants you encounter. Their chemical constituents can help prime your mood and influence how you feel. Lavender, for example, is calming through raising levels of the neurotransmitter sero-tonin, whereas rosemary is stimulating through boosting levels of dopamine and acetylcholine. The smell of roses can help with stress through reducing levels of adrenaline and prolonging the activity of relaxing endorphins.

When we connect to a natural setting through all of our senses and are fully immersed in our experiences, our fight-or-flight response is automatically reduced, and the parasympathetic system is activated, leading to a state of restorative restfulness.

2

Awesome Walking

'With gratitude, optimism is sustainable.'
Michael J. Fox on CBS News *Sunday Morning* show

Recently, I was involved in a campaign to raise money for the mental health charity Mind. My job was to get people walking in nature. Specifically, I was encouraging them to pull on their wet weather gear in the darker winter months, when the benefits of being outside are just as impactful as in spring and summer, but the mood slightly less inviting. For some. Not for me. I love a winter walk on a crisp chilly day, and I enjoy walking in the rain because I think about the droplets scrubbing the polluted atmosphere clean before hitting the ground.

My colleagues at Go Outdoors (a company specialising in outdoor activities and kit) simultaneously conducted some research with the charity, and there were a few interesting findings. Of the two thousand people questioned, two-thirds said that daily outdoor walks are one of the lasting legacies of our pandemic lockdowns. A walk allowed them to take time for themselves, they said, and almost forty per cent thought it made them more appreciative of the world around them.

Is that gratitude? Is it awe? Is it just relief at having a bit of time and space for oneself? Full disclosure: for me, it's all three!

I think this trinity of emotions – gratitude, awe and wonder – merge in the mind for most of us. We use them interchangeably, both the labels and the ideas, but in science they can be individually defined.

Awe, wonder, gratitude

Awe and wonder are more interlinked than awe and gratitude. If you want a proper distinction, try this one from Ulrich Weger, a German professor of psychology and psychotherapy, and his fellow German Johannes Wagemann, a professor of consciousness research. They explain it like this: 'Wonder inspires the wish to understand; awe inspires the wish to let shine.' In a nutshell, when feeling awe, we take a step back and observe, allowing the thing evoking awe to work its magic on us. Wonder is more likely to make us want to ask questions of something or join in.

A call from the wild

Dacher Keltner is a psychology professor at the University of California (Berkeley) and a best-selling author. He defines awe as 'a feeling of being in the presence of vast things we don't understand', and believes it's essential to human development.

For him, awe is an ennobling experience that can foster creativity and collaboration. You can read about his lived experience of awe and his study of it in his most recent book, *Awe: The Transformative Power of Everyday Wonder*.

Professor Keltner recognises the awesomeness of nature, which he calls 'wild awe'. His book asks: 'How might we make the case that we have a biological need for wild awe, a need on a par with our needs for protein-rich food, thermoregulation, sleep, oxygen and water? Or the more social needs, like being loved, cared for, touched, esteemed and respected?'

He describes our bodies as behaving like an antenna for wild awe when they're outdoors in nature – and that includes setting out for a walk on a gloomy winter's day.

When it's cold and dark, you might not fancy suiting and booting up, but according to the professor:

> *It is hard to imagine a single thing you can do that is better for your body and mind than finding awe outdoors. Doing so leads to the reduced likelihood of cardiovascular disease, respiratory disease, diabetes, depression, anxiety and cancer. It reduces asthma in children. It leads to reductions in everyday aches and pains, allergies, vertigo and eczema.*
>
> *Our bodies respond to healthy doses of awe-inspiring nature like we respond to a delicious and nutritious meal, a good sleep, a quenching drink of water or an uplifting gathering with friends and family: we feel nourished, strengthened, empowered and alive.*

Nature snacking

Using nature to nourish me is something I've learned to do, and I think gratitude creeps into these 'nature snacks' too.

I take a break from my desk regularly now, consciously standing up and heading outside if I can, even if it's only for five minutes. A quick walk or a bounce on some grass, some purposeful breaths, eyes wide and gazing towards the sky – I promise you, it gives me a boost. It's like having a sip of strong herbal tea or a shot of caffeine.

I make sure I listen to the sounds and look around with intention, soaking up whatever is outside. If I hear a bird chirp, or watch a cloud float past me, these small things make me smile. That's gratitude tiptoeing in. I land back at my desk refreshed and refocused – nourished, if you will.

The last time I did this was just now, before I wrote this

paragraph; I took a quick spin around the garden to watch the sun dipping away (another day ending), and heard a robin belting out his song over the grumble of a big motorbike vibrating at nearby traffic lights.

'How can these two things exist in the same universe?' I thought to myself, full of wonder at the diversity of my local environment.

Nature offers endless opportunities for us to be awestruck, contributing to our own wellness, while also reinforcing our innate connection to the natural world.

Trees – friends with benefits

I can't think of a better example of just how amazing nature can be than the discoveries brought to light by the work of Suzanne Simard. When she was a little girl, Suzanne became fascinated with trees, particularly the roots and fungi – odd, but perhaps not so surprising for someone raised in the Monashee Mountains of British Columbia, the westernmost province of Canada. Her grandfather was a horse logger who taught her the 'quiet cohesive ways of the woods', and following in his footsteps, she was inspired to study forestry.

She began working in the business of commercial tree-harvesting, but it soon became apparent that modern industrialised methods of forest management were brutal, and that didn't sit well with Suzanne. Trees were no longer being selectively cut, which was how her grandfather had operated. In time, the spraying and hacking of the aspens and birches would prove too much for her to bear, and she quit and went back to school.

Fast-forward to 1997, when a female scientist announced an incredible discovery on the cover of the prestigious publication *Nature*: trees can talk to each other.

She proved that they communicate via an intricate system of fungal wires known as mycorrhizal networks, passing nutrients and carbon back and forth depending on each tree's need. We see the reproductive organs of these threads when we walk through woodlands and forests. They're mushrooms. And this 'wood wide web' is so dense that there can be hundreds of kilometres of them twisting, winding and binding in the earth beneath our feet. Those infinite biological pathways connect trees and allow the forest to behave like a single organism.

The scientist was Suzanne Simard, and few scholars have made such an impact with a PhD thesis. This discovery – and her subsequent revelation that 'Mother Trees' exist, playing a matriarchal role in forests, taking care of trees in need and specifically their own kin if extra help is required – has fundamentally changed the way we understand trees.

Also, as Suzanne hoped, it has changed the way forests are managed. Or at least, it should do.

'I say to the trees, "I hope I'm helping,"' she admits.

You will have gathered by now that as much as I admire the beauty and poetry of nature and its rich emotional and physical rewards, I also like the hard science that comes courtesy of academics such as Dacher Keltner and Suzanne Simard. It reassures me that all these amazing benefits are real (something our ancestors instinctively knew).

Both scientifically and poetically, learning that trees talk to each other blew my mind. It has the same effect on most other people, too.

In October 2022, I was sitting next to Reverend Richard Coles in a ramshackle radio studio at Broadcasting House in London, co-hosting Radio 4's Saturday morning show (imaginatively called *Saturday Live*). We received a call from Jez, a sound recordist who'd responded to our shout-out for 'landmark nature moments'.

Jez had a recording of the inner sounds of the root system of a cherry birch tree, recorded when he was in East Yorkshire. We were all sitting in a circle as if we were at an AA meeting, with funny bulbous microphones dangling from the ceiling above. It was one of the most memorable, unique noises I've ever heard, like crackly water. If I use the words 'noisy sap', does that help you to imagine it? (You can go to the BBC Sounds app and listen for real if you want.)

Our guests were the singer-songwriter Craig David, the former stylist and now best-selling author Susannah Constantine, the nature-loving YouTuber Kwesia (also known as City Girl), and Sandy Nairne, a former director of the Tate Gallery and the current deputy chair of the National Trust. Each of them sat back and listened in wonder, and probably awe, too. It's hard to know which word to pick.

The small things are the Big Things

Suzanne Simard is now a professor of forest ecology at the University of British Columbia. I shared her story because it is so remarkable. It not only leaves me in awe of the complexity of nature, and this exceptional human who followed a hunch, but it also speaks to the connectivity of nature and us.

Trees need each other; it's a symbiotic relationship. We need each other. We need the trees. And so we circle back to the thought that awe stimulates us and makes us feel connected, as well as driving people to what Dacher Keltner calls 'paradigm-shifting discoveries'.

I'm left with the belief that it's essential to have the capacity for awe, so we can lead richer, more fulfilled lives with the potential for significant personal change and growth.

When I think of some of the most wonder-filled and awe-inspiring moments in my lifetime so far (apart from childbirth), they have mostly been in nature. In all of these instances, I have been inspired to understand more about the place or the moment (as Weger and Wagemann suggested earlier), or to step back mentally and let the magic of the experience wash over me. It makes me feel very 'present', something that is hard to achieve in today's world.

Crunching up an icy Blencathra with friends during a winter visit to the Lake District, against the backdrop of a bright blue sky . . .

Creeping towards the edge of the Grand Canyon and standing aghast at its vastness, holding my mother's hand, after an unforgettable trip to Las Vegas . . .

Stroking the leaf of a *Mimosa pudica* (which means 'shy' or 'bashful' in Latin) on a hike through the verdant countryside of Bel Ombre in Mauritius, and watching it shrink and fold inwards when touched, only to reopen a few minutes later . . .

These are moments I will never forget. They continue to fill me with awe and wonder, and I feel profound gratitude to have experienced them.

But it's important to note they're separated by decades.

If we're lucky and live to the age of eighty, we'll have had 28,000 days on Earth. (That's the equivalent of *four thousand weeks*, the name of the book written by Oliver Burkeman, who I'll be talking to later in this chapter.) It means we'll only have standout experiences like this once every five or ten years.

There will be weddings, significant birthdays, promotions, friends' successes to celebrate, mountains conquered, pink sunsets in the company of loved ones – but we'll be fortunate if these moments tally a dozen across our lifetimes. So what about all the other days, weeks and years? What are they? Barren, because they are shorn of some blockbuster moment?

They shouldn't be.

What I've learned is that we have to find joy in the ordinary, in the little things, and I have created a saying – 'The small things are the Big Things' – as a kind of shorthand for myself.

Smiles exchanged with strangers on the street, acts of kindness, the warmth of winter sun on your face (which is gorgeously called 'apricity'), trying to count the hundreds of stomata on the surface of a leaf – these all matter. So do moments of laughter with your children, giggling at something silly with your partner, and talking about nothing with your best friend for an hour.

These are the small things which are actually Big Things, and we will experience far more of them than all those 'standout' occasions. The little things are the stepping stones on which we cross the ordinary days of our lives – all 28,000 of them, *if* we live to eighty – and we should be very, very grateful.

Louise's story: One step at a time

The day before Louise Trewern changed her life, she walked a total of twenty-five steps, from her bed to her chair to the loo.

She weighed twenty-five stone, suffered osteoarthritis and fibromyalgia, and had been on opioid painkillers for more than a decade. By the end, she had to be admitted to hospital to be weaned off a massive daily dose of Oxycontin plus another opioid painkiller, a morphine liquid, diazepam (Valium), and antidepressants, all prescribed by her doctor.

To help manage the side effects of withdrawal, her consultant instructed Louise to pace the ward, triggering endorphins with their natural pain-killing properties.

'Suddenly, I have my earphones in and I am going up and down, and up and down the ward,' Louise tells me from her home in Torquay. 'When he came back in the next day, I had done two thousand five hundred steps, listening to an indie band from Southampton.'

She graduated to a wheeled walking frame, a wide one to accommodate her bulk, and from there to a walking stick. Soon, she was able to walk unaided, and she and her wife went out every day with a packed lunch, a flask and their wet weather gear. 'It became my new addiction,' she says. Welcome to the club!

In time, Louise, now fifty-five, a mother of four and grandmother of six, would be well enough to start work with for a not-for-profit company supporting people living with pain. Today, she travels around the UK telling her story, inspiring others to manage their own health without the kind of chemical cosh she lived under.

She also set up a couple of guided walks for other people in her situation. One is three-quarters of a mile around a tree-lined lake with twenty-two benches to rest on; the other is two miles long, with the promise of a community café at the end. Both are thriving.

'I'm not sure there are words to describe my gratitude at being able to get outside and back into nature,' she says. 'I climbed Hay Tor on Dartmoor for the first time in more than twenty years, and started swimming in the sea again – though I call what I do swimbling, because it's the equivalent of an amble, not too far and not too fast.

'On the day my brother got married, he wanted us all to climb a mountain in Wales in the morning and be back in time for his wedding that afternoon. The feeling I got at the top was unbelievable. He tried to send a car to collect me on the way down, but I refused. I said, "No, I am going to finish this." And I did – with ten minutes to spare!

'A year after I managed to come off opioids, I dyed my hair a colour called Pink Pizazz – I wanted all the music, all the sparkles, all the jewellery, all the make-up. I'm grateful for everything.'

Get grateful

Like Louise, I have learned the art of gratitude these past few years. It's something I've started practising with a vengeance since my cancer diagnosis, but here's an odd thing: it can be tricky at first, because our brains are wired towards the negative.

This is called a negativity bias, and the outcome is that we tend to focus on negative experiences, not positive ones, which means gratitude doesn't come naturally.

If I ask you to recall your most memorable journey into work, what springs to mind? It's probably the day you got stuck for seven hours in a traffic jam on the motorway, or the time you got taken off the train and loaded on to a bus to get to your destination. But what about the morning when everything went smoothly? You got half an hour to read your book on the bus, then you had a nice chat with the person sitting next to you, made it to the office on time and had a really nice cuppa.

We tend to more easily forget those non-events, the days when things run just fine, and there's a reason for that.

Historically, our negativity bias played an important role in our evolution. The perception of threat was critical to human survival; it was how our ancestors stayed vigilant against the myriad environmental dangers that surrounded them. This means that in the twenty-first century, gratitude – giving thanks for all the good things in our lives – requires attention and intention.

So today, I write a gratitude journal several times a week. I find it steadies the ship.

Practising gratitude requires us to slow down long enough to think and reflect. Our old Roman friend Cicero thought it was the 'mother of all human feelings', and it's true that focusing on what you do have, not what you don't, puts you in a different place mentally.

That cascade of positive feelings has a physical impact, too. Research in the past few decades has established an overwhelming connection between gratitude and good health, reduced stress, improved sleep and enhanced emotional awareness.

In the professional environment, gratitude is linked to more vitality, energy and enthusiasm. It encourages us to work harder and helps build commitment. We all like our good work to be acknowledged, don't we? (It certainly makes me feel fuzzy with happiness.) Grateful workers are more efficient, more productive and more responsible. Expressing gratitude in the workplace helps to build bonds and trigger the positive feelings associated with that. So tell your boss!

When we express and receive gratitude, our brains release dopamine and serotonin, two important neurotransmitters responsible for emotions that make us feel good. By consciously practising gratitude every day, we can help firm up these neural pathways to create more positivity within ourselves.

That means gratitude builds on itself. The brain changes with experience, so the more that gratitude is practised, the more it learns to tune in to the positive things in the world. Sadly, like our muscles, this tissue in the brain often begins to decrease in late adulthood, even before symptoms of cognitive dysfunction appear. So get gratituding, quick!

Gratitude interventions

Counting blessings or gratitude journals Try writing down five things you're grateful for daily or weekly (I do this roughly four times a week). On the everyday days, you will have to reach into your mind to find good things, but they will be there – no matter how small. A bright sky, a thrush singing its heart out in the park, a message from a friend . . . remember, the small things are the Big Things.

Three good things In a 2005 study, American psychologist Martin Seligman (well known in the scientific community for his theories on positive psychology and well-being) tested a variation of the gratitude journal where participants had to write down three things that went well during the day and also identify the causes of those good things.[1] This required extra thought and more time, which is one of the good side effects of doing these interventions, I think; it forces you to slow down and consider life.

Mental subtraction This is when you imagine what life would be like if a positive event had not occurred. In one set of experiments, people who interrogated themselves about this or that not happening reported that their mood improved. It became known as the 'George Bailey effect', named after the character James Stewart played in *It's A Wonderful Life*, the classic 1946 movie that's on the TV every Christmas. If we want to get closer to the current century, we could call it the *Sliding Doors* effect, after the film in which Gwyneth Paltrow plays a woman whose life works out very differently depending on whether she catches or misses a train. Hmm, even that film was back in 1998! Anyway, you get the idea . . .

Gratitude letters Write and deliver a letter of gratitude, in person, to someone you've never properly thanked. This is a gratitude *and* visitation practice. Extra points, surely?

Death reflection Reflecting on your own death can also increase gratitude. Our existence is a continuous state that we can easily take for granted – and usually do. Reflecting on your death might sound morbid, but it could increase your appreciation for life. (Obviously, I don't recommend this for anyone who is terminally ill or dealing with the terminal illness of a loved one. It is very good, however, for those times when you are in a rough patch and have the words 'Why me?' stuck on a loop in your head.)

Experiential consumption Spend money on experiences rather than things. One study found that people felt and expressed more gratitude following an experience than they did after giving or receiving an object.[2] The obvious advantage of enjoying something like a concert, a weekend retreat or a visit to an exhibition is that you can do this with someone and build a good memory. This is your green light to go out and have a good time!

Maude's story: Meditation, mindfulness and gratitude

Maude Hirst was a successful actress. She first appeared in BBC's *The Tudors* followed by a starring role as Helga in four series of *Vikings*, a blockbuster hit worldwide. She could have had her pick of acting jobs, headed to Hollywood, perhaps, or become a mainstay of British TV drama. Instead, she quit show business and the red carpet in favour of meditation and mindfulness.

Maude is now a full-time meditation facilitator (and trained yoga teacher) with her own mindfulness business called EnergyRise (see maudehirst.co.uk). This has become a global community that specialises in making meditation accessible to everyone. She is grateful daily for her transition from a career that she felt wasn't a true expression of herself, to one that fulfils and inspires her.

'The success of *Vikings* made people start taking me more seriously as an actor – it would get me in the room for a lot of other big productions,' she recalls. 'But I started realising people were more interested in my character, Helga, than me. There was a fascination around success, but it was not necessarily about me as a person.'

The overwhelming end of a major relationship proved a turning point. 'My relationship fell apart and the career I thought I'd wanted for all those years had not brought me happiness and fulfilment. I'd been acting since I was ten and I had never stopped to ask myself: am I actually happy? I felt I was in a void.'

She took a holiday, a wellness break, and was transported by her discovery of meditation. It had such a massive impact on Maude that it changed the course of her life. She went on a journey of self-discovery, completed numerous mindfulness training courses, including a ten-day silent meditation retreat, and subsequently pivoted into a full-time career building her EnergyRise community.

'I was so grateful to discover meditation, and when you're grateful, I think you invite more good things into your life. Today I work with gratitude all the time. I think that, unknowingly, we can be [caught] in a negative internal dialogue. Gratitude switches the dial and makes you start looking at all the things in your life that *are* working. The more you do that, the more you look for the brilliant stuff, the more your life shifts into a peaceful, grateful existence.

'I always felt I was hidden behind scripts and cameras. Being competitive didn't come naturally to me. This version of me, now – maybe on the outside, doesn't look as glitzy but from the inside, it feels a million times more glamorous, because I feel assured about who I am.

'I did a podcast this morning where I mentioned that I love the phrase: "We're human beings, not human doings." Gratitude helps you to be in the moment; it tells you that you're enough without having to chase the next thing in order to find happiness.

'I'm in my mid-thirties now and for the first time I am settled in myself. The funny thing is I'm not sure I would have found [this] if I hadn't had that big life blow-up. I might never have been curious enough to make the change. So I am even grateful to the bad things that led me to this path. Meditation and gratitude changed my life and I believe they can do the same for you too.'

Wonderlost

Our understanding of the science of awe and gratitude is new – but our knowledge of the benefits we draw from them is not. Back in the fifties, the pioneering environmentalist Rachel Carson spoke and wrote about the human preoccupation with things that are 'artificial and alienate us from sources of our strength'. She was referring to the kind of turbo-charged indoor life that takes us away from sources of wild awe and their manifest benefits, as outlined by Professor Keltner.

In the July 1956 issue of *Woman's Home Companion*, Carson wrote an essay called 'Help Your Child To Wonder'. In it, she describes some of her outdoor escapades with her nephew Roger, whom she raised after her sister died. She wanted him and other children to acquire an 'indestructible sense of wonder, at the world, something which will be an antidote against boredom and disenchantment' in their later years.

Her hope was that, if we have our sense of awe and wonder ignited in childhood, then we will carry it throughout our lives. But in order to do that, children need to spend time in green spaces. They need access to nature, and mentors to show them the way.

Most of us now live in towns and cities, and forty per cent of children never play outdoors at all. You may remember some headlines from a few years ago, which revealed that three-quarters of British children spend less time outdoors than the country's prison inmates.

The *Oxford Junior Dictionary* makes understanding what's happened as easy as ABC. The *OJD* is aimed at seven-year-olds, and over the last few decades our increasing detachment from nature has been revealed both by the words it includes and the words it leaves out.

A is not for acorn, but for 'attachment'; buttercups have been replaced with 'blogs' and there is no room for catkins, although there is space for 'chat room'. Words that were part of my childhood vernacular have been dropped to make way for new ones that represent a very different idea of early years.

Cauliflowers, chestnuts and clovers have been axed, but children can 'cut and paste' and use 'broadband' technology to search for their favourite 'celebrity'. Herons, herrings and kingfishers are no more; larks have disappeared from the pages of the dictionary (and, sadly, largely from our skies). Magpies are just as unlucky.

Leopards, lobsters and minnows mean too little in today's world to count. Mussels have shrunk to nothing; newts, otters and oysters have been replaced by 'MP3 players', 'voicemail' and 'databases'. Even nectar is left to the imagination. (The word 'nectar' is derived from *nektar*, the Greek name for the drink of the gods, which conferred immortality on any mortal lucky enough to enjoy it. That's right – you can't even get eternal life into the *OJD* these days.)

There have been petitions and denouncements. This deletion of nature prompted the brilliant nature writer Robert McFarlane to create a beautiful book called *The Lost Words*, filled with illustrations and poetry that beautifully and mournfully depict many of them. With the book's artist, Jackie Morris, he embarked on a country-wide crusade visiting schools to protest in favour of parsnips and liquorice, tulips and poppies and – some of my favourites – the wrens.

It seems madness to me that when we know how much we need wild awe in our lives, we are letting our children – and ourselves – slide ever deeper into a digital world of screens and social media instead.

Clocking on

While social media plays a crucial role in our lives, it shouldn't be where we spend the majority of our four thousand weeks – that needs to be among people and in nature, walking yourself happy.

I spoke to Oliver Burkeman about his book, whose very title reminds us that our lives are finite. *Four Thousand Weeks: Time and How to Use It* is about making the most of your time on Earth and living a life of meaning.

When we spoke, Oliver was at his new home in Yorkshire. He has just moved back from New York to be closer to family and to nature, as he shows me when he swivels his computer screen so I can see what he can see – the Yorkshire hills stretching into the distance. (I know, I know – more screens, but at least we are using them to connect and talk *about* nature!) He starts by amiably agreeing with something I hear a lot: that people think they don't have *time* to sit in the morning light or take a daily walk.

'I'd say they're quite right.' He laughs. 'But this notion that if you cut out time spent in nature you'll get to the bottom of your to-do list, it's delusional. We are finite, yet we live in this world of infinite possibilities, infinite potential obligations, and infinite to-do lists. What liberates you to spend time outside in the sunshine or walking by a river or enjoying a forest is choosing to neglect the other things you could be doing in that moment.'

He gets out into the spectacular landscape where he now lives almost every day. He loves the sense of being at one with it, and finds natural awe 'essential' for keeping his working life in perspective. 'I don't think of myself as a crazed megalomanic narcissist, but it's really easy in the course of a day to look at your dramas, stresses and deadlines, and think that the world hinges on them, when [it] really doesn't. Getting outside helps you recognise that we are quite small in the cosmic scheme of things, and there's something calming and grounding in that.'

Oliver is at ease with the idea that this means other things will go undone – in fact, he finds joy in missing out. 'Forgoing something makes your choice to do something else have more meaning. Being a finite human is all about making sacrifices,' he muses, which is a pretty big thought for a midweek afternoon.

Since he's an expert in the science of time management, I ask his advice for finding and making time – in this case, for nature, health and wellness.

'If you can't afford half an hour a day, then do ten minutes, and if you haven't got ten minutes, do five. A minute or two or three is so much more than zero because it crosses the gap from not doing something to doing it.'

Then he adds something seemingly counterintuitive: 'It's actually surprisingly useful to stop after whatever time you've said you'll do. So if you've planned five minutes, don't let it turn into twenty-five minutes, even though that sounds a lot more virtuous. Doing something for a shorter period makes you more excited to get back to it the next time; it can be highly motivating.'

The other thing he counsels against is trying too hard to be 'in the present' because it's self-defeating – and even he is not immune.

He remembers the night he was lucky enough to see the northern lights while on a journalistic assignment in the far north of Canada. The sky had been stubbornly dark until the very end of his trip, when he was woken by the couple in the next-door hut banging on his door to tell him the aurora borealis was alive.

'It was totally amazing, an extraordinary display of the northern lights, but as I was staring at it, I found myself thinking, "Oh, it looks like a screensaver on one of those old-fashioned PCs with all the green lines bouncing around . . ."'

It happened, he thinks, because he was trying so much to be 'in the moment' that he was failing, thinking about his own thoughts and watching his own reactions instead.

'Living more fully in the present may simply be a matter of finally realising that you never had any other option [than] to be here now,' he writes in his book.[3]

Oliver has an interesting relationship with gratitude because of his keen understanding of time and the fact that it is finite for us all. He has kept a gratitude journal in the past, but these days depends on unguided meditation.

He says: 'There's a theologian, who I quote in *Four Thousand Weeks*, who refers to this idea of being on the receiving end of God's gifts and God's love. I think you can enjoy that in a secular way, too. There's something about just getting to be here, alive, and getting to experience what you experience. It's not a forceful insistence that you feel gratitude for this or that. For me, it's about reminding myself there is this constant flood of experiences and people coming at me, and I don't have to do anything because it's coming anyway.'

Like me, he thinks it's the small things that are the Big Things.

As he points out, what gets encoded in memory is the new and the different, which is why we remember a three-day mini-break but not the last three days of our ordinary life. Since you can't be on a mini-break the entire time, the alternative route to the same destination (happiness, inspiration, nourishment) is to extract more sensory data out of your every day.

Joyriding

How to find gratitude in the smallest of places

If you accept that the small things are really the big things, then it begs the question: can you find gratitude in unlikely places – your own kitchen sink, for example? Broadcaster Angela Scanlon seems to have found a way. She takes a similar approach to Oliver Burkeman, giving grateful thanks as she goes about ordinary tasks, such as putting crisp new sheets on her bed or cooking a meal for her family. It's been transformative for her happiness and well-being and professionally has given rise to her podcast *Thanks A Million* and her memoir *Joyrider* (joyriding is what she calls 'gratitude in motion').

Angela lost her footing a little, growing up in a busy Irish household of four sisters. 'I felt really overwhelmed by things other people take in their stride,' she admits. 'I tried to strangle and squash and stuff down big feelings by narrowing my focus.' First that was with food, which became 'a way for me to control a world that felt out of control to me'. Then it became work and her pursuit of higher-profile television jobs, which she thought might fill the emotional hole inside her.

'The turning point was when I had my first daughter and I had to stay at home. With motherhood, there was nowhere for me to hide any more. It was a very, very stark realisation that what I had been doing to make myself feel better wasn't working.'

She hunted for something else, and chose gratitude simply

because she could make it work within the confines of her hectic schedule. 'Sometimes you feel you are adding to a to-do list that's already insurmountable, but gratitude fits into your life; it can be a silent internal thing or three nice things you see that you write into the notes on your phone.

'I think we can be dismissive of simple things, and that's how I was with gratitude. "This feels really simple. Where's the magic bullet? Where's the expensive machine? Why am I not chasing something shinier, more Instagrammable?"

'Working on your gratitude muscles [is] like . . . trying to work on [your] physical fitness. Nobody wants to hear "eat less and move more", they're like, "No, no, no, give me a big, complicated, fabulous thing that I can focus on, then drop after a month and blame everybody else."

'Gratitude is about the small things and seeing them all the time. It can feel like a cliché, but they're the magic and fabric of life.'

Can you find the G-spot?

I'm a relative newbie on the Gratitude Train, but I can tell you that shifting my perspective and using it as a tool during my cancer diagnosis changed everything for me.

A cancer diagnosis is one of the worst things that can happen in a lifetime. I felt a genuine, bursting, panicky, tight emotional pain deep in my chest. I needed to release the grip it had on me so I could handle whatever else was to happen in the coming months.

Focusing on all the good in the situation – and in my life – helped me escape the overwhelm.

I expressed gratitude for all the sound advice I had available to me, my excellent medical team, my tree to talk to (see page 151), my children to love, my in-built resilience, and my mum and dad still being here to parent me. The list goes on: my lovely doodling pencil, a sip of fresh, cold water . . . They are the small things that became my Big Things.

Practising gratitude means searching for them, intent on bringing them to the fore. Focus on what you *do* have, not what you don't. You are shifting the way you think, conditioning your mind so that this new state becomes habit.

I would encourage you to give it a go, because gratitude sweetens the smallest moments. You might want to try this little exercise.

Do try this at home: Walking with gratitude

Happy tree, happy me

Later in this book you'll meet my trees. I do my morning breathwork perched on my bathroom windowsill looking out over a London plane and a horse chestnut tree. I say hello when I pop my head out the window and after each session I say thank you. I also walk every day, even when I'm away filming, but when I'm home it's usually to one of my local parks.

As I move along the familiar routes I say thank you to the trees along the way: lime, hawthorn, silver birch, ash (sadly not around for much longer because of the fatal ash dieback disease), oak and cherry blossom. I'm grateful to them all for keeping our soils healthy and helping to purify the disastrous London air. By understanding their importance and by expressing my gratitude, I'm also connecting to nature, which makes me care more. And that's the secret. Caring. If you care, you want to do your best by that tree landscape (or person) and that gives you a sense of purpose and belonging. So next time you are wandering along your local canal path, or through your patch of nearby green space, or even just on the way to the station for your commute to work, try expressing some thanks and gratitude to your regulars.

Walking it Off: Nutrition

'Never eat more than you can lift.'
Miss Piggy

Food is an incredibly divisive topic today, and if you are not a follower of Hippocrates' school of thought – 'Let food be thy medicine' – then you might want to skip this chapter.

Actually, don't – you may need this bit the most.

Alongside how to optimise our 25,000 breaths, walking as many steps as possible and getting the right amount of sleep, what we *choose* to eat three times a day is one of the single most important decisions we can make regarding our health.

Until a couple of years ago, I didn't give much serious thought to how and what I ate. Because of my work on consumer shows like *Watchdog, Kill It, Cook It, Eat It* and *Countryfile*, I've learned how food systems work and I've always been conscious of food quality, but I didn't plan my meals, calculate how much protein I was eating or count my veggies.

My career has been about making walking, outdoor and travel shows for television; beautiful, scenic programmes showing off stunning landscapes and colourful characters. But without fail, the two questions I get asked most aren't about any of that. Instead, they are: 'What walking boots do you wear?' and 'What snacks do you keep in your backpack?'

The answer to the second was always: a bacon sandwich (brekky on the move); milk chocolate; millionaire's shortbread (especially in the Lake District, where it's really good); flapjack; a ham or Cheddar sandwich; crisps; a bag of wine gums (red ones only) and an apple. Sometimes we'd be on location for eighteen days straight, so that's what I'd eat . . . for eighteen days straight. Every night at the end of filming, the crew, me included, would descend on some lovely country pub and tuck into homemade pie, chunky chips, a big old steak or bangers and mash. Then pudding – always pudding. Brownies, ice cream, apple pie and custard, chocolate mousse, sticky toffee pudding, blackberry crumble . . . my mouth is watering just typing this.

But when I look at that list now, I also shudder. Let's start with the chips. Fried foods carry heart risks, in part because they provoke inflammation and they're often high in sodium as well as harmful saturated fats.[1] The oil in which foods are fried commercially is often heated again and again. This can generate a variety of compounds, many of which have been reported as carcinogenic.[2] The humble sausage (soooo good with mash and onion gravy) is made with processed meat, and science says eating that raises your risk of early death. It's all to do with nitrates, which, once in the body, can be converted into cancer-causing compounds. They occur naturally in red meat, but are frequently added during meat-processing as a preservative.[3] Sausages are high in fat and salt, too. And all red meat contains a pigment called haems, which is broken down in the gut to form compounds (called N-nitroso compounds or NOCs), which are also known to cause cancer.

Then there's all the sugar. Sugar comes in many forms, and is hidden in foods that you wouldn't expect. It's not just in sweets, cakes and biscuits, but things like sauces, soups, fruit juices and meat products (wait until you read about Subway's sandwiches on page 70).

The average American now consumes approximately 126g of sugar a day. That is about ten tablespoons. We are not far behind in the UK, packing away approximately 93g, or around seven and a half tablespoons a day.[4] There's a huge body of evidence showing the damage too much sugar does to human cardio-metabolic health.[5]

I certainly ate more than the recommended daily allowance of 24–30g of sugar – I was well known for my sweet tooth. And now? I don't. I stopped cold turkey and switched to dark choco-late (anything over seventy per cent cocoa) and nut butters, which are a good replacement for sweet flavours (hazelnut rather than peanut). This was just one part of a huge overhaul of my diet which I undertook after my cancer diagnosis and mastectomy.

Despite being a chocoholic, it only took a fortnight to re-educate my taste buds. Today, when I do have a slice of cake or taste the kids' homemade cookies, I make sure it's after a full meal, never on an empty stomach. If you eat your veggies first, the fibre coats your small intestine, leading to a lower glucose spike. That's better for you.

Quitting sugar saw me lose a lot of weight. I shrank to 56kg, which is unhealthy for someone who's five foot eight inches tall. I've put several kilos back on, but I still get trolled for being skinny on social media. You can be body-shamed whatever your size, and I've always had a slim build.

The other thing I am pulled up for most often on Instagram is when I talk about the link between cancer and obesity.

The UK has 15 million obese people, and that number is rising. As I said, I know what it's like to be body-shamed, and I am not here to do that. I am highlighting the fact that Cancer Research UK says being overweight or obese is the second biggest cause of cancer in the UK (it causes more than one in twenty cancer cases), and the risk is higher the more overweight you are.[6]

Extra fat doesn't just sit there, it's an active substance that sends toxic messages to other parts of your body. Sometimes, those messages encourage other cells to divide abnormally. Sometimes that causes cancer. Saying this gets me a lot of push-back (and clearly this is only one risk factor: I don't fall into this category, and I got cancer), but pretending it's not true doesn't make it any less dangerous.

Weirdly, I always thought I was healthy. Although I never meal-planned, I ate vegetables (mostly overcooked and dripping in oil); I ate salads (covered in dressing); and I ate good-quality meat.

Then I had to educate myself and re-evaluate.

What I learned is that 'good foods' don't balance out 'bad foods' and you can't exercise your way out of a poor diet. Oh, and you *do* need to meal plan. What's required is a Gordon Ramsay style approach, where you look at what you eat across the week and say, 'That's rubbish, that's rubbish and that's rubbish,' and fix your family's menu accordingly. It took me a year to get control of my kitchen and to be confident I could cook a nutritious meal for myself and my children in a hurry.

I'm very proud of that – though I do miss the chips.

The eighty/twenty rule

Chips are not off the menu completely, however. I now cook and eat by the same eighty/twenty rule I use for exercise and sleep. For eighty per cent of the time, I eat healthy, whole foods, and the other twenty per cent of the time, I treat myself or accept that I am doing my best in the circumstances. Somebody's birthday? Of course I will have a slice of cake. But if I am out at an Italian restaurant, I won't routinely order the zucchini fritters Mum and I used to love, and pasta's pretty much off the menu too. It's too soon post-cancer for me to look at food that isn't healthy, and tuck in anyway.

So these days, up a mountain, you'll find me with an egg, an avocado, berries, perhaps a plant-based yoghurt, and some seeds and nuts to sustain me. I might have some leftovers from last night's protein in there, too. You can see some of my favourite snacks opposite. I am not vegetarian; I've adopted a 'plant-facing' diet, and occasionally I eat small fish such as mackerel, a little high-welfare beef or free-range organic chicken. (My meat comes from Pipers Farm near Exeter. I discovered it while filming *Kill It, Cook It, Eat It,* and I have stayed loyal.)

Some of my favourite snacks

- An egg, hard-boiled, free-range farm sourced where possible
- Blueberries, blackberries and raspberries, in any combination, whatever I have in my fridge
- A pot of plant-based yoghurt, normally coconut based, packed with pumpkin and sesame seeds, with a touch of vanilla essence for extra sweetness if required
- Something sweet pre-prepared, such as homemade muffins or pancakes made with almond, coconut or cassava flour
- An avocado mash with coriander, lemon and spring onions – on its own or with the pancakes and muffins
- Mackerel or sardines in lemon juice with fennel seeds
- A mixed pot of pecan and pine nuts
- The best dark chocolate available, anything over seventy-five per cent cocoa. My favourite is dark chocolate buttons!

Growing up in the 1970s, I remember my Greek mama feeding my big sister Gina and me liver and onions, avocados, mushrooms on toast and salmon. (I hated salmon and I'm still not a huge fan, ditto sardines. That said, I made myself eat sardines recently, and established they are juuuust about OK with lemon and caraway or fennel seeds. I have accepted that when you are refuelling with food – as opposed to relishing a meal with family and friends – every mouthful doesn't have to be an 'event' or give you the same dopamine hit as a cheese toastie.)

The Bradburys ate a lot of food that reflected Mama Mou's heritage, family favourites such as Mediterranean stews and moussaka. I remember spending many happy hours rolling keftedes (Greek meatballs). Every family has their own recipe, their own tradition, and thinks theirs are the best. Ours definitely are, delicately flavoured with fresh mint, which I know now is packed full of vitamins and minerals.

Mum cooked everything from scratch. She always warned us about pesticides and made us wash our fruit and veg, which remains the rule in my kitchen today. Mostly, though, my dad grew vegetables for the family table in our back garden in Rutland. There were runner beans and potatoes and carrots and Jerusalem artichokes, with which he made his legendary Fart-i-Choke soup.

These recipes have been reproduced straight out of Mum's kitchen files.

Keftedes

    450g (1 lb) minced beef or lamb
    1 onion, finely chopped
    3 slices of bread, soaked in red wine (these days I would substitute shelled hemp seed or grated cauliflower for the bread, as I try to limit my wheat intake)
    1 egg, beaten
    a handful of mint, well chopped
    a healthy dose of cinnamon
    salt and pepper
    grated Parmesan cheese, to taste

Mix together all the ingredients, adding water or wine to bind (the mixture must be moist). Leave to rest for at least an hour, then roll into small balls and fry gently in hot olive oil until cooked through. Do not burn!

Fart-i-choke Soup (I'll let you guess why we nicknamed it this . . .)

    450g (1 lb) Jerusalem artichokes, well scrubbed and cut into small chunks
    lemon juice to taste

1 onion, chopped
50g (2oz) butter
570ml (1 pint) chicken stock
1 glass white wine
salt and pepper

Soak the artichokes in water and lemon juice for an hour or more.

Sauté the onion in butter until soft. Drain the artichokes and stir them into the onion mixture. Add the chicken stock and white wine and simmer for 30 minutes.

Liquidise then season to taste and cool in the fridge or serve immediately. Finish by adding a splash of double cream or dollop of plant-based crème fraiche. Garnish with chopped parsley. Yum.

Staying hydrated

Now, before we dive in to the importance of nutrition, we need to talk about hydration. I could write a whole chapter on the type and quality of the water we drink, but that's a rabbit hole for another book. Let's stick to how much 'clean' fluid we should be taking in on a daily basis.

The estimates vary from six to eight glasses a day, but at the time of writing, Andrew Huberman (the neuroscientist and tenured professor of neurobiology and ophthalmology at Stanford School of Medicine, and host of the *Huberman Lab* podcast) is suggesting the optimal amount of fluid intake is, on average, 8oz (236ml) for every hour you're awake in the first ten hours of your day. Consumption can then taper down. Note, though, that this doesn't allow for fluids lost during exercise, nor for being in a very hot climate.

I know, I know: you're recoiling from the page, shouting, 'No way!', but actually it's not that much – about three-quarters of a glass, every hour. You don't have to do this *on* the hour – plus, coffee and tea count as fluids, as do soft drinks, but remember that soft drinks can be very high in sugar and/or strange chemicals so I would encourage you to avoid them. In total, this recommendation works out at approximately 2 litres of fluid a day.

How are you doing?

Historically, I think I've come up a little short, but since I've learned more about the benefits of staying properly hydrated, I'm more focused on reaching this goal.

At this point, I should highlight that it is possible to *over*hydrate. Hyponatremia is caused by having too much water in your body, diluting your sodium levels and watering down your blood. Hyponatremia can also occur when we lose too much sodium by going overboard with alcohol or using diuretics, when we suffer severe diarrhoea, or if we take some medications including antidepressants and painkillers. Our bodies need sodium for fluid balance, blood pressure control and the proper functioning of nerves and muscles – so there is such a thing as too much water.

But let's be honest, usually we drink too little – and that matters, because humans are mostly made of water (between seventy and ninety per cent). Being dehydrated can reduce our strength and endurance, alongside our cognitive performance, including memory, focus and creative thinking.

Dr Andy Galpin, who has often appeared on Andrew Huberman's podcast, explains that, in terms of dehydration, 'Two per cent alone is enough to reduce accuracy and performance. Once you start getting into three, four or five per cent dehydration, you start having a significant reduction in blood volume, and that's incredibly important for endurance. Your blood becomes viscous, it's hard to pump through and you're going to start having all kinds of issues.'

Without proper hydration, none of the cells in your body can function. So let's get glugging. Cheers.

Gut instinct

I grew up on a pretty healthy diet and I don't feel as if my habits have changed; it's more that the food around me has changed. It's become processed, packaged and pinged in the microwave. It's also become available 24/7, so it's normal to eat what you like, when you like, instead of having three balanced meals a day.

How on earth did that happen?

I decided to speak to Professor Tim Spector, OBE. Tim is a professor of genetic epidemiology at King's College, and the world's best-known scientist on gut health. His books, *The Diet Myth* (2015), *Spoon-Fed* (2020) and *Food for Life: The New Science of Eating Well* (2022), have changed the national conversation about how we eat. He is a world-renowned expert on the human microbiome, the 2kg of bacteria and bugs that live inside each of us and dictate our health.

Like me, he thought he ate reasonably well and was fit and healthy. Then he had a stroke walking uphill on a pair of skis in the Alps when he was in his early fifties (at the time of writing, he is sixty-five).

If he hadn't tackled his nutrition after that wake-up call, he reckons that today he would be 10kg heavier, have higher blood pressure, probably be taking statins for his cholesterol – and would definitely not be skiing up any mountains. Actually, he thinks he would have retired instead of turning his attention to the microbiome and becoming one of the top hundred most frequently cited scientists on the planet.

Tim is no a killjoy when it comes to food. He believes eating is a basic human pleasure and is a sucker for a 'nice, slightly burned, crispy lasagne where I can scrape the cheese off the sides of the dish'. His guilty pleasure is a bottomless bowl of cashew nuts and he only learned to love beetroot once he'd turned fifty. In short, he sounds like any of us.

His life's work – studying identical twins and asking why one might get cancer or become depressed while the other remained well – would play a significant part in his groundbreaking study of nutrition. It was only when he realised that identical twins, genetic clones of each other, had vastly different gut health, he understood that what we eat counts for more than our genetic inheritance.

I begin by taking a step back and asking him to explain the microbiome, because it's a pretty new area of science and is linked with many elements of our health.

'It's hard to visualise, but imagine we've discovered a new organ, a virtual organ, in your body,' he says. 'It's a similar size to your liver and weighs as much as your brain. It's in the lower part of your intestines, your colon.

'What this bag of microbes does, essentially, is to act as a whole series of mini-pharmacies. They convert the chemicals that reach your colon into other chemicals: vitamins, hormones, neuro-chemicals for your brain, and all the signals you need for your immune system to work well. We can't exist without them.

'It's a unique microbial garden. I use the analogy of a garden because it's made up of lots of different species; you've got bacteria in there, fungi, parasites. A healthy microbiome is like an abundant garden with as many different species as possible. An unhealthy one is like a wasteland, very few species, little diversity. Those mini-pharmacies have run out of stock.

'In the West we've lost half of the diversity that we had maybe a hundred years ago, and there are many species we're never getting back.

'The antibiotics we take kill off harmless bystanders in the microbiome; so does spending [more] time in sterile city environments and less outside, walking in the woods, getting dirty, gardening, or [working] on farms, as our ancestors used to do. Finally, the big thing is eating ultra-processed foods with nasty chemicals that our microbes react badly to – processed foods deprive them of fibre and bombard them with artificial substances such as sweeteners and emulsifiers.

'The loss of gut microbes, which started a hundred years ago, has accelerated since the 1970s in tandem with the rise of processed food.'

That doesn't come as a shock to me. Food has changed – and not for the better – since I was a kid eating my greens in the seventies.

Our lives today are lived in a higher gear than they were half a century ago. The food industry has adapted to meet our new needs and nudge them in a direction that does more for their bottom line than our health. I'm going to leave the nuts and berries of food science to specialists like Tim – I would recommend reading any of his books to further your knowledge – but you only have to look in your fridge or kitchen cupboard to see the evidence with your own eyes.

There are so many added ingredients: fillers to bulk up foods (made of things like cellulose and olestra that the human body can't digest); emulsifiers to enhance texture and extend shelf-life (they're linked to increased inflammatory bowel diseases); and antibiotics. The overuse of antibiotics in animals is contributing to the rising threat of antibiotic resistance caused by our own dependence on them.

Tim says around fifty-seven per cent of an adult's diet and seventy per cent of a child's in Britain today is made up of processed food. We know to be wary of treats like biscuits and cake, but he's more worried about the less exciting items in our shopping baskets: the supermarket breads and breakfast cereals and convenience foods that have been 'stuck together in a factory using glue and the genius of scientists to make them look like food, and taste great'.

'I'm in favour of things like Coca-Cola and Pepsi,' he adds, somewhat surprisingly, 'because no one has ever said they're healthy. It's pretty obvious what you're having when you buy a Coke. Have one occasionally. Enjoy it. It's all the other stuff, the low-fat, low-calorie foods that people have every day, thinking they're healthy when they're not. We have the most ultra-processed food of any country in Europe, and it's getting worse every single year.'

The National Food Survey

Defra, the government's Department for Environment, Food and Rural Affairs, offers a fascinating insight into how we, as a nation, have changed the way we eat. A cross-section of British families keep a detailed weekly food and drink diary for something called the National Food Survey. It's been in existence for more than seventy years so it shows clearly how our habits have evolved. Back in 2016, the government published reports from the 1940s and wartime rationing, through to the 1970s and the advent of fridges and freezers in British homes.

In the 1940s, gardens and allotments provided more than ninety-two per cent of fruit and vegetables used in country households, a figure that rose to ninety-eight per cent in the summer. In towns and cities, gardens and allotments accounted for twelve per cent of the fruit and vegetables in the winter and forty-nine per cent in the summer

By the 1970s, however, we wanted faster easier food such as frozen peas, which were newly popular. Flour, a kitchen staple, was less in evidence because fridges and freezers meant we didn't have to cook from scratch every day.

We had started eating out and snacking on the go, too: in 1952 almost half of British households ate exclusively at home, but by 1983 we were eating on average three meals a week in a café or a restaurant. I bet it's many times that today – and what if you add in our Deliveroo culture where you can stay in your house or apartment but send out for an egg sandwich?

What I find most revealing – both for what it says about our eating habits and the food industry – is that in the 1940s, around a third of our household income was spent on food. Today, it's just twelve per cent. I think that shows just how much we have devalued food, in terms of both its nutritional and its monetary value.

We don't view it as precious any more – and we should.

Let's return to Tim's work on twins, which led to one of what he calls his 'Ah-ha!' moments in researching the microbiome.

'I'd been studying twins for thirty years,' he tells me, 'but it was only when I got to look at the gut microbes inside them for the first time that I saw something which was really different. Knowing we all have individual gut microbes, and that they might be interacting differently with our genes and our environment – that was the first thing which told me this could be an amazing discovery. It explains a lot of the mysteries around medicine – and what we've got wrong.'

His second 'Ah-ha' moment was understanding that 'we're all highly individual when it comes to our responses to food'. That means if I eat a blueberry muffin, it will have an entirely different effect on my body than it would on yours if you ate the same thing. Those differences between us, Tim proved, are almost all down to lifestyle.

He says: 'When it comes to nutrition, genes have a very small part to play. Only thirty per cent of our response to sugar is controlled by genes, and less than five per cent of our response to fat. And overall, general inflammation is not very genetic at all. It means that you can do something about it, you can change your gut microbes. You can, in a way, change your destiny. What you can't do is blame your parents.'

There are exceptions, and they are coffee, alcohol and milk. We all know people who get tipsy on half a glass of wine, and people who, like me once upon a time, can drink a bottle and still talk sense (hmm . . . maybe). That's genetic. Some people can down a pint of milk with no problem, while the lactose in it will make others feel queasy. That's genetic too. And there's an enzyme in coffee to which some of us are highly sensitive, and others aren't. So you can thank your genes for your tolerance to double espressos, as well.

Apart from these three, you are what you eat, pretty much.

'Big Food' Tim believes, is now a bit like 'Big Tobacco' in the 1970s, when cigarettes lower in tar, nicotine and carbon monoxide were marketed as being better for you. He says food standards won't improve until they become part of the political agenda, and since this isn't happening yet, we all have to take control of our own diets.

'You absolutely cannot wait for the government,' he warns. 'They aren't going to change anytime soon. They're worried about the reaction if they put food prices up by so much as a penny. They don't think long term. They don't think of the huge health price we and our children are going to pay.'

Globally, poor nutrition still accounts for 11 million deaths every year.[7] It adds more to the global burden of ill health than sex, drugs, alcohol and tobacco combined. The consumption of vegetables, legumes, fish, nuts, seeds and fruits is way below the level recommended by the World Health Organization, and we are eating too much fat, processed meat, salt and sugar.

But given the amount of processed food on our supermarket shelves, this isn't entirely our fault. Take bread, for example. We've called it the staff of life since biblical times because it's a human staple. Yet these days, some bread isn't even *bread* any more. In 2020, the Irish Supreme Court ruled that the rolls used by sandwich chain Subway (the ones used in heated sarnies) contained too much sugar to be labelled as bread.

Subway rolls also made the headlines in 2014 when the company announced it was removing 'azodicarbonamide' (ADA) from its rolls. ADA is used to whiten flour and improve the condition of dough, but since its other function is in the manufacture of vinyl foam products like yoga mats and carpet underlay, it's affectionately known as the 'yoga mat' chemical. To this day, it's allowed in baked goods in America but banned in the UK and the European Union.

I don't know about you, but I prefer not to eat my yoga mat, not even in child's pose. (For the non-yogis among you, that's where you are face down on the mat, forehead, nose and chin so close you could lick it.) Sadly, there are a lot of horror stories like this. As Tim points out, the zero-fat, zero-calorie, zero-sugar versions of fizzy drinks marketed as 'healthy' alternatives to the full-fat versions are sweetened with substances that are by-products from the petrol industry. Yum.

Hands up – I'm guilty. I have eaten and drunk – and enjoyed – my fair share of junk in the past. Sadly, there's photographic evidence. I remember one epic *Countryfile* shoot that had started at 5am, filming wildlife at dawn, and ran through until the light gave out in the evening. I was heading home with Matt Baker, sharing the driving, both of us ravenous. Eventually, we found a motorway service station with a burger bar. As I gobbled my food (no other word for it), a fan took a picture and posted it on Twitter with a caption saying something like, 'Well, she looks hungry . . .' and there I was, wild-eyed, mayo dribbling down on my chin, half a burger in my mouth, for all the world to see.

At the time of writing, I am back on the road filming a series in Ireland for Channel 4. This time, I am travelling with a bag of supplements and my team knows that no matter what, I will start my day with organic vegetables such as broccoli, cabbage and red leaves.

I couldn't resist asking Tim his opinion of my post-cancer diet. Apparently, it puts me in the healthiest twenty per cent of people in the country, in terms of a happy microbiome. It took me more than a year to get there, but it's possible to make signif-icant change in as little as a fortnight.

 ## Julia's typical meals then and now

Then

Breakfast: a bowl of cereal and a slice of toasted supermarket bread, with jam, or a crumpet with honey

Elevenses: a doughnut or dunking biscuits dipped into sweet tea or coffee

Lunch: a light pasta dish, a supermarket sandwich or cheese on toast

Tea time: a chocolate bar or chocolate biscuit, perhaps a bag of crisps as a pick me up

Dinner: shepherd's pie, spaghetti Bolognese, pizza, meat or fish and a couple of vegetables with a side helping of starchy carbs such as chips or mashed potatoes

Pudding (always): ice cream or a bucket of popcorn with Maltesers tossed in (while watching TV)

Now

Breakfast (not eaten until 10am or afterwards): a plate of multi-coloured steamed, mixed seasonal vegetables, always including broccoli, sprouts or cauliflower, drizzled in extra virgin olive oil, sprinkled with fennel seeds and chopped fresh herbs, with a side of protein (either avocado, fish or leftover meat from the night before)

Second course of brekkie: a bowl of mixed berries, blackberries, blueberries, raspberries, covered in hemp seeds, flax seeds, pecan nuts, pine nuts, with dark cocoa nibs as an extra crunch and treat, topped off with a natural flavour plant-based yoghurt or sometimes full-fat Greek yoghurt; weak coconut milk latte, with a splash of MCT oil (coconut oil) and nootropic mushroom powder (a mix of mushroom powders) stirred in

Lunch: a colourful mixed leaf salad drizzled with extra virgin olive oil and apple cider vinegar sprinkled with pine nuts and a side of steamed or cold fish or a hard-boiled or scrambled free-range egg

Dinner: typically something like cauliflower rice smothered in a lemon and tarragon turkey Bolognese made creamy with a plant-based crème fraiche, with a side of steamed, mixed vegetables and/or beetroot OR a coconut-based Thai vegetable curry

Pudding (now only sometimes, not always): a handful of blueberries and a cheeky square or two of dark chocolate or dark chocolate buttons, all eaten in one sitting, not in front of the telly and at least four hours before bedtime

Easy, healthy swaps

Here are the main swaps I have made to avoid packaged convenience foods:

Instead of traditional pasta try courgette 'noodles' or cauliflower 'rice' for a tasty base. I got used to these new flavours very quickly.

Instead of wheat flour in bread, cakes, pancakes and biscuits I now use cassava, coconut, fava bean or almond flour as the main ingredient.

Instead of refined, processed sugar I sometimes add dates and Greek honey (of course) or vanilla essence.

Snack attack? In weak moments, I reach for blueberries or a couple of squares of good-quality dark chocolate

Tim advises adding fruit, veg, nuts and seeds to your diet, and getting your hands on fermented foods such as kefir, kombucha and kimchi.

And we have to stop judging food by its calories.

'They're a nonsense,' he says. 'As a way of teaching people how to eat more healthily, that should be scrapped. It's not about calories. It's not about fats and carbs and protein, either. It's about food quality. It's about your own personal time of life: whether you're going through the menopause; whether you are suffering from an illness; whether you're male or female; whether you're exercising – there are so many variables. Your sleep last night dictates how big your sugar spike will be when you eat your normal breakfast, how hungry you'll feel, whether you're more likely to pick bread than a yoghurt.'

As he says: 'Each time you eat, think of nourishing your gut microbes, and that way you can't go far wrong. And remember, with a hundred trillion microbes inside us, you're never going to eat alone again!'

'Eating windows'

I speak a lot in this book about the pressure of our 24/7 lifestyles, and unfortunately we now eat 24/7, too. If you live in a city, you can have anything delivered, any time. If you're travelling, convenience food is always available. Even if you're at home with a cooked-from-scratch meal on the hob, you might be waiting to eat with a partner or kids getting in late.

We've dropped our sensible breakfast, lunch and dinner routine. Supper might be the main meal of the day, and it might come just before bed. We graze. We snack. We treat ourselves . . . and you know what I'm going to say, don't you?

We shouldn't.

I love food. But the human digestive system puts a huge strain on the rest of the body, and it's not good for us if it's in constant use. It needs to be allowed to do its job and then rest up, because otherwise it gets in the way of other critical bodily functions.

So you might want to look at the idea of what are known as 'eating windows'.

This is where you give yourself a window of just ten or twelve hours within every twenty-four for eating your meals. (You can try a fourteen-hour window if the shorter span is too much to manage.) Some people who are super organised and have good self-discipline can get down to eight hours, with brunch at 10am and dinner at 6pm. I'm usually somewhere between the two.

This is properly known as time restricted eating (TRE), and it means you don't have to restrict how much you eat, just when – though obviously avoiding ultra-processed food is a good idea.

A 2022 report in *Endocrine Reviews*, published by the Oxford University Press, detailed the outcome of experiments on animals and people who consistently ate within a twelve-hour window.

It said early trials on humans 'have reported promising results in reducing the risk for obesity, diabetes, and cardiovascular diseases. Epidemiological studies have indicated that maintaining a consistent long overnight fast . . . can significantly reduce risks for chronic diseases.'

In trials on animals, without limiting calories, TRE prevented or reduced the severity of several metabolic diseases, including obesity, glucose intolerance, fatty liver disease, dyslipidaemia (an abnormal amount of lipids in the blood), and age-related decline in heart health.

Most of us eat for about fifteen hours across the day, sometimes more if you get the munchies late at night. This is loading your poor body with physiological stress. Eating windows are a straightforward way to solve that, so start late, finish early and . . . do you want my top tip? Go for a ten-minute walk (nothing vigorous) after you've eaten. When you are up, out and moving, it will help you stop craving food again. And if you can't manage ten minutes, then try for three, it's definitely better than nothing.

Plus it puts some distance between you and the biscuit tin.

Our ancestral health

Navigating a new way of eating introduced me to Pauline Cox MSc, founder of the brilliantly named Sow & Arrow, a play on bow and arrow. She believes humans should eat congruently with ancestral health – the 'Sow' refers to the plants and 'Arrow' to pasture-raised meat. Her practice – I hesitate to call it a business – began life as a café and shop in Clevedon in North Somerset, with a focus on anti-inflammatory, low-carb food. When Pauline wrote a book and developed her online teaching during the pandemic, Sow & Arrow found a national audience.

Pauline has degrees in Anatomical Science and Physiotherapy, and a Masters in both Nutrition and Integrative Medicine. Her first book, *Primal Living in a Modern World*, was published in 2020, and her second *Hungry Woman*, eating for good health, happiness and hormones, was released in June 2023.

She believes we all have the innate capacity to support healing within ourselves, and that we can build pockets of optimal nutrition into everyday life.

Pauline doesn't think we lack the willpower or the desire to change – just the knowledge of where to start and how to work with our physiology, not against it.

In this next section, she addresses four significant areas of nutritional health, and suggests easy switches to improve them. She also explains how walking is critical to a healthy bowel and why we also need to get outside to increase our ability to build dopamine and serotonin, and reinforce our immune systems.

Pauline's four pillars for creating a robust foundation of health

Pillar one: Balancing blood sugars

Imagine the feeling of the first bite of your favourite biscuit. The blissful sensation hits hard and fast, but as the last few crumbs disappear, you're left with a sense of longing. You give in and swiftly swallow another few biscuits. The heady highs are soon followed by a feeling of needing more.

Food manufacturers are well aware of the physiological changes happening in our brains and bloodstreams as we dive deeper into the biscuit barrel, finding ourselves uncontrollably finishing the packet and then wondering how it happened.

We are not inherently greedy or lacking in self-control. This comes down to much more than willpower. The simple biscuit is doing more than tickling your taste buds; it is hitting your brain chemistry hard and sending dopamine levels rocketing. Couple this with the surge in blood sugars, and it's not difficult to see how addictive certain foods can be.

The short-term longing for more isn't the real problem, it's the impact these blood sugar-spiking, dopamine-stimulating foods have on our hormones, inflammatory levels and overall health.

The bloodstream typically has one teaspoon of blood glucose circulating – until we eat. What we eat will determine the magnitude in the rise of our blood sugars. A diet high in blood-sugar-spiking foods will, over time, see serious consequences at a cellular level, which manifest as very common symptoms synonymous with modern living.

When blood sugars rise as a consequence of eating, trusty insulin jumps into action, knocking on the door of our muscle cells, brain cells and other body cells to open up and let glucose in to be used as fuel. Blood glucose cannot remain in the bloodstream, as it is damaging to the tissues of the body.

As we continue eating our blood-sugar-spiking diet, year upon year, insulin becomes overworked and eventually resistant to the instruction to mop up more sugar. More insulin is needed to open the doors of the cells and shunt the glucose out of the bloodstream. A state of insulin resistance emerges. It manifests as hypertension, weight gain, fatigue, systemic inflammation and common hormonal imbalances, such as polycystic ovary syndrome.

Diet is the easiest way we can impact our glucose levels and insulin sensitivity.

Here are some simple ways to keep blood sugars balanced:

• Become conscious of carb intake
Carbs are not bad – however, the amount and type of carbs we eat is key. Carbs are the biggest offenders when it comes to spiking blood sugars. Reduce foods that spike blood sugars, such as refined carbs: pastas, flour-based biscuits, cakes and pastries. Even 'healthier' grains, such as oats, can spike blood

sugars if your glucose sensitivity is poor. Focus on obtaining carbs from sources such as root vegetables, seeds and nuts, particularly if you suspect you have poor tolerance to glucose and insulin resistance (suggested by high blood pressure, easy and/or stubborn weight gain, poor hip-to-waist ratio (weight gain around the middle), sugar cravings or getting 'hangry').

• Veg out on veggies

Fill up on a variety of colourful veggies and salads, including leafy greens, cruciferous veggies such as cauliflower, broccoli and cabbage, and cucumbers, tomatoes and peppers. Douse them in olive oil for extra goodness. (Although I always ate vegetables, if they were stir-fried in oil, the oil was generally highly processed vegetable and seed oil, which I now try to avoid. These days I use olive, coconut or avocado oil. Little tip: you can actually stir-fry vegetables beautifully with just a dash of water.)

• Seek out high-quality protein

Protein is essential for growth and repair, as well as building the brain hormones serotonin and dopamine. We need a steady supply of quality protein, and without it, we can experience a loss of muscle mass. This is bad news for your balance, bone health and metabolism. Make sure you eat adequate protein daily, from sources such as oily fish, eggs, natural yoghurt, cottage cheese and goat's cheese (and tempeh, nuts and seeds if you are vegan). Protein will help you feel fuller for longer, as well as supporting healthy hair, skin, lean muscle mass and brain chemistry.

• Eat healthy fats

Fats often get a bad rap, but the truth is, fats are our friends! We need fats for many functions in the body, but not all fats are created equal. Processed foods containing high levels of fats to avoid include pastries, cakes, biscuits and fast food. Healthy fats include those found in oily fish, such as salmon, mackerel, sardines and anchovies, as well as in olives, avocados and eggs. These fats are beneficial to our mental and physical well-being.

• Get moving

Our hungry muscles need energy as we get moving; even a simple walk sees our thigh muscles shouting out for instant fuel. The habit of going for a walk after eating means the muscle cells mop up blood sugars, rapidly bringing down the blood sugar spike that may have otherwise stayed high for hours.

• Sleep well

The quality and quantity of sleep we have affects our hunger hormones, blood sugar sensitivity and cravings. Sleep makes a big difference to the impact foods have on our blood glucose levels. Ensuring you have a good night's sleep is foundational to good health.

Pillar two: Reducing inflammation

Inflammation is not inherently bad; in fact, it's an essential part of self-defence from invading pathogens. It's the chronic, persistent drip of low-level inflammation that becomes damaging and destructive to many tissues of the body. The persistent state of inflammation causes collateral damage that has become all too familiar in our modern society: chronic inflammatory diseases such as type 2 diabetes, heart disorders, respiratory diseases and cancer. Chronic inflammation sees the infiltration of inflammatory cells into tissues such as blood vessel walls, and the liver, lungs and brain.

The signs and symptoms of chronic inflammation are often accepted as part of modern living. We excuse the feelings of fatigue, low mood or aches as down to our age or the fact that we're always busy. However, these symptoms can be radically improved when chronic inflammation is turned off and tissues start to recover.

Common signs and symptoms of chronic inflammation include:

- low mood, anxiety or even depression
- feeling tired all the time, or insomnia
- digestive issues, such as constipation or loose stools
- weight gain or weight loss
- joint pain, muscle pain, migraines or general body pain

Changing your diet is one simple way to impact inflammation levels. What we eat can significantly influence inflammation, switching off pro-inflammatory pathways and exerting an anti-inflammatory effect.

• Fats

Omega-3 and omega-6 fatty acids are known as essential fatty acids. They are 'essential' because we cannot make them ourselves and so must obtain them from our diet. Their roles are wide-ranging, from being part of the structural integrity of our cellular membranes, to supporting a healthy immune system, brain, nervous system and cardiovascular system.

In an ideal world, we would have a balanced ratio of omega-3 and omega-6 fats in our diets. While both are essential, omega-3 tends to support reducing inflammation, while omega-6 fatty acids increase inflammatory levels. When our intake of omega-3 fatty acids is low and our intake of omega-6 is high, this mismatch can increase chronic inflammation levels. Ensuring you have plenty of omega-3 fatty acids in your diet, from sources such as oily fish, eggs, chia seeds, flax and walnuts, can help to reduce this mismatch.

• Fibre

Fibre-rich food is a must. Not only does fibre support bowel health and friendly gut microbes, but it also scores highly on the anti-inflammatory charts. Fibre-rich foods will help you feel fuller for longer by reducing overeating, and also support hormonal balance through keeping bowel movements regular.

Eat plenty of fibrous, colourful veggies, such as carrots, cauliflower, broccoli, beetroot, Brussels sprouts, avocados and artichokes.

• Friendly bacteria

Familiarising yourself with fermented foods and finding a way to incorporate a dollop of sauerkraut into your day will help to transform your gut microbiome and potentially your health. The gut is a microclimate of its own, housing a secret world of bacteria, fungi and viruses, all working diligently to support the health of the host – you! Imbalance in gut bacteria can be a primary source of inflammation.

Keep the bacteria in balance by eating a diet rich in colourful, fibrous foods to support a healthy gut microbiome, and try to eat a forkful of fermented food every day as professor Tim Spector also recommends. There are so many tasty choices when it comes to fermented foods, from turmeric sauerkraut to fermented beetroot. Not only is sauerkraut a rich source of beneficial bacteria and fibre, it is also a super source of vitamin C.

Pillar three: Detoxification

What goes in must come out! The effective elimination of waste is just as important as what we eat, and this is reflected in the health of the liver and bowels. Giving the liver a little attention pays dividends. It is the workhorse of the body. Anything we eat or drink is digested in the gut and taken to the liver via the bloodstream for processing. Toxins found in the environment, and in our food system, medication and alcohol, are all processed and detoxified by the hard-working liver.

The liver also plays a crucial role in fat-metabolism through producing an important substance called bile. While not the sexiest of subjects, bile should have its own award for best supporting act, since it is crucial for the breakdown of fats and the absorption of fat-soluble nutrients, such as vitamins A, D, E and K. Bile also carries processed toxins away from the liver ready for excretion.

Supporting a healthy liver and bile flow all contributes to the effective removal of toxins, used-up hormones such as oestrogen, and healthy bowel movements, all of which reduce the likelihood of waste being reabsorbed back into the body.

A healthy liver starts with you giving your liver the nutrients needed to do its job; these include B vitamins, amino acids, sulphur-rich foods and antioxidants. Leafy greens, bitter foods (such as rocket and nettle), protein, and sulphur-rich foods (such as broccoli, cauliflower, garlic, leeks and onions) all support healthy detoxification and bile flow. The fibre in these delicious foods also adds to the elimination pathways being supported through healthy bowel movements.

Constipation affects individuals of all ages; however, premenopausal women are estimated to be two to three times more likely to suffer than men.

Walking also improves bowel health, by reducing constipation through the effects of upright posture and gravity, muscular contraction and the increased release of gastrointestinal hormones.

Pillar four: Building a robust nervous system

The nervous system has a profound impact on our physical health through the cascade of stress hormones released, so supporting the nervous system has become an increasingly important consideration. Eating for mental well-being is very much in line with eating for gut health – what's good for the gut is good for the brain!

The brain is the hungriest organ in the body. It demands fuel and nutrients in order to function optimally, and if its demands are not met, the brain will throw a diva fit and you will know all about it. Poor focus, brain fog, low mood, insomnia, anxiety, cravings, apathy, irritability . . . the brain will run through a conveyor belt of emotions to let you know that it needs nutrients, *right now!*

With so many of us overfed but undernourished, the brain has a hard time getting across the message that it needs more. This often manifests through cravings. The brain and gut have a very sophisticated means of communicating with each other. Neurones in the gut sense the presence of key nutrients needed by the demanding brain, such as omega-3 fatty acids and amino acids from protein. If these key nutrients are not being sensed by the gut and relayed to the brain, then the brain will keep pumping out the message that we need to eat more: 'Keep going . . . we don't have what we need yet!'

Eating a wholefood, nutrient-dense diet will support the brain, nervous system and mental well-being.

And please don't forget to go for a walk! The synthesis of our neurotransmitters dopamine and serotonin depends on key nutrients, including B vitamins, amino acids and vitamin D. You get vitamin D mainly from exposure to sunlight (though small amounts can also be found in our diets). But exposure to sunlight doesn't only increase our levels of vitamin D – when sunlight enters the eye, hitting the back of the retina, serotonin levels rise. Low levels of daylight and low activity reduce serotonin and dopamine levels, so a walk is a natural way to boost them both and increase your feelings of happiness, motivation and confidence.

Food culture

It's clear my Greek heritage was helpful in creating the solid food foundation in childhood, which I built on post-cancer with the help of Pauline and Dr Nasha Winters, author of *The Metabolic Approach to Cancer*. Both experts have guided me through my body's needs and helped me create a new, healthier menu for the second half of my life.

Tim Spector thinks the absence of a 'strong food culture' in the UK is one of the reasons why Britons now eat so much processed food.

'A strong food culture means cooking and eating what our grandparents did,' he explains. 'Grandparents pass recipes down to their kids and grandkids, and say, "This is our family dish, so don't change it." When someone comes along and suggests using margarine rather than olive oil – well, a Greek family just wouldn't do it. Same for Italy, same for Spain, same for France, same for Portugal. In the 1980s, when doctors came out and said, "Butter is bad for you, change to margarine," here in the UK, we all behaved like lemmings. There was no grandmother to say: "That's not true." I was doing my doctor bit, thinking, hmm, you know . . . but I'm married to a Belgian, and she wasn't taken in; she refused to change. And it turns out, she was absolutely right.'

In the absence of this intergenerational wisdom, we can't turn to our GPs, either. Medical students don't study nutrition, or if they do, it's only for a few hours. Some studies suggest the average UK medical student only gets two or three hours' training in the subject across their entire medical learning experience. (Tim points out you might learn more about nutrition from a decent personal trainer than your doctor.)

This is madness, since Pauline and other nutritionists are clear you can heal or reverse some health issues with food before you need drugs. Nutrition is key to treating many common chronic diseases, such as heart disease and type 2 diabetes, and it's playing an increasing role in building our immune response to viruses like Covid-19, too.

Plus, as Pauline says, it's not just about physical health – it's also about mental health.

Tim agrees. 'The brain–gut axis is really important,' he explains. 'We know from hundreds of studies that anxiety and depression and stress in humans cause a disordered gut microbiome. If you take a stressed human's poo and you put it into mice [via faecal transplant], you can make them anxious and stressed. A Mediterranean diet has been shown in randomised trials to work at least as well as antidepressants – and, in several studies, better.

'I think the whole idea about depression, anxiety [and] stress, being treated through diet and probiotics, is one of the most exciting areas in this field,' Tim says.

Another area for the professor's future research, and one of particular interest to me, is the impact of the natural environment – getting out and being in nature. Different environments – woodlands, parks, green spaces – expose us to different microbes. 'If you walk [on a treadmill] in a gym, that may not be nearly as good as walking in the park or out in the country at weekends,' Tim affirms.

 ## How to test your microbiome

How can you tell if your microbiome needs help? Bloating, pain after meals, constipation and not having a poo at least every two days (preferably once a day) are all signs your microbiome is struggling.

If you want to know more, you can visit Tim's ZOE healthy study (www.joinzoe.com) and take the 'Blue Poop' test. You make a fluorescent blue muffin in your kitchen at home, eat it, and, in the professor's words, 'count how many hours it takes until it appears, miraculously, giving you a shock, a day or two later in the toilet'. The test is an accurate measure of how long it takes food to pass through your body, and that correlates very well with your gut health. The average in the UK is about twenty-eight hours. It should be less than twenty, really.

Dig your vegetables

But look, it's not all bad news. The drift away from field-to-fork produce is slowing, and more and more of us are searching for a way back. Justine Paul runs a string of farmers' markets across East Anglia, including one in the Suffolk village of Lavenham (if you're a *Harry Potter* fan, you'll know it as Godric's Hollow from the films). It was voted the best farmers' market in the UK by the Farm Retail Association in 2022. Nothing sold there comes from more than thirty miles away, and most of it has been grown, baked, brewed or butchered by the person manning the stall.

When Justine launched her business in 2008, farmers' markets attracted an older demographic having a 'day out' rather than doing a big shop. Today, the majority of her customers are local, committed and much younger.

'It's because they care about the provenance of their food,' she says. 'If it's pork, they want to know where the pig's been raised, what it's been fed, where it was killed, how it was butchered, who butchered it. They want to meet the farmer and ask those questions, to know there is no middleman or middlewoman.

'Good quality and higher food standards, they go hand in hand with provenance. A decade ago, one of the things thrown at me was that farmers' markets were expensive. That comes up less often these days, many people are willing to pay more for local seasonal food that isn't wrapped in plastic and polystyrene. That's the trend nationally – quality and durability are prized.'

So artisan and local producers are fighting back, one turnip at a time, and the rest of us are increasingly growing our own too: yes, Britain's allotmenteers are on the rise.

At the end of World War Two, in an era of rationing and food shortages, there were 1.4 million allotments in this country, according to the National Allotment Society. By 1997, there were just 265,000, and 42,500 of those were vacant. Today, in contrast, you can't get one for love nor money in some areas.

The longest recorded waiting time for a plot was eighteen years and three months, in Camden in north London. That was for an allotment that was handed over – finally – in 2021. Nottingham City claims the crown for the longest list: 6,845 gardeners were waiting for their little patch of green in 2021. People are so desperate to get growing that councils are splitting plots, yet demand is still outstripping supply and waiting lists continue to grow.

Why? Well, the association estimates it costs just £247 a year on average to cultivate a 250-metre square plot, while the value of its produce could be around £2,000. But it's not about the price of fruit and veg. The association also acknowledges the savings from less time spent off work sick, fewer trips to doctors and dentists, and the mental health benefits of a community endeavour (belonging to a community is an important part of human well-being).

Here's a little bit of food history for you. The majority of allotments were developed under the Defence of the Realm Act of 1916, which permitted local authorities to commandeer land that would be good for growing during World War One.

We're fighting a different kind of battle today, one for good, unprocessed food. But guess what? You can still join the war effort and dig for victory on an allotment, in your back garden, up on your balcony, or in a window box if that's what you've got. You may not achieve a perfect diet – who will? – but don't let that be the enemy of eating better, getting soil on your hands, and being outdoors.

Stepping out

In lots of Mediterranean countries it is very common to take a walk – an old-fashioned promenade – after dinner for its social and health benefits. I now have a quick walk (less than ten minutes, sometimes only two or three) after every meal, to help my digestion, reduce my blood glucose spikes and add to my daily step count. It is also a great opportunity to catch up with loved ones. Obviously this might not be possible every single time we eat, in which case I make sure I do something active such as lunges or exercises with my arms in the air – clapping my hands above my head and below my waist.

4

Walking and Sleep

'A ruffled mind makes a restless pillow.'
Charlotte Brontë, *The Professor*

I didn't think much about sleep when I was younger. If you haven't hit your fifties yet, you might not think about it much, either. It's just that time we spend in bed (when we're not having sex) in between the interesting bits of life, right? Turns out, no!

Confession time. I have been guilty of self-harm when it comes to my nocturnal habits, but, in mitigation, I didn't know exactly how much damage I was doing. You lose a lot more than Zs when you don't sleep well – and the science of sleep has just started to tell us exactly *how* important it is.

There is such a thing as sleep diversity. Some people need more or less than others, and this changes throughout our lives. Anything between six and eleven hours a night is within the margins of normal. But, even allowing for this, more and more of us can only dream of getting a good night. In the last seventy years, we've lost more than an hour's sleep per night – in the 1940s and 1950s we enjoyed more than eight hours, today we get an average of 6.7–6.8 hours a night. This is not without consequences for some of us.

Our wise ancestors

Our wise ancestors, as ever, had a view. The ancient Greeks were great believers in the restorative power of sleep. Hypnos, the god of sleep, was seen as the remover of pain, suffering and sorrow. The Greeks were confident that what sleep does for the body, dreams do for the mind, enabling it to rest and regenerate.

Egyptian cotton bedlinen may be a famous luxury, but the contribution of ancient Egypt to the field of sleep medicine goes beyond 1,000 thread-count sheets. Sleep was used as a method of healing in special Egyptian sleep temples, which were hospitals of sorts, healing a variety of ailments.

The Greeks also had them, built in honour of Asclepius, the Greek god of medicine (not to be confused with the father of medicine, Hippocrates, who gets several mentions of his own in this book). They were filled with healing prayers and, um, non-venomous snakes. If you look closely, you'll find snakes on all sorts of medical symbols to this day, including the emblems of the World Health Organization and the US Army Medical Corps. Non-venomous or otherwise, snakes of any kind wouldn't help *me* sleep – of that, I'm certain.

There's an old Irish proverb (and since I was born in Dublin, I feel qualified to use it): 'A good laugh and a long sleep are the best cure in the doctor's book.' Like all proverbs, it's rooted in truth. Sleep deprivation affects everything from mental health and memory to immunity against coughs and colds. It's linked to all manner of serious chronic illnesses, including Alzheimer's, cancer and cardiovascular complaints.

Let's take just one of those, Alzheimer's. Sleep helps detox-ify the brain by flushing out the rubbish that builds up during our waking hours. These waste products drain from the brain along a series of channels surrounding our blood vessels. This is called the glymphatic system. In a 2013 study, scientists found the glymphatic system helped remove a toxic protein called beta-amyloid from brain tissue. Beta-amyloid is known to accumulate in the brains of patients with Alzheimer's disease.[1]

The science of sleep has advanced enormously in the past two decades, and I'm not going to try to explain it all here. Brilliant scientists, such as Professor Matthew Walker and Professor Russell Foster, have written wonderful books on the subject and, after you've finished *Walk Yourself Happy*, I would urge you to buy, borrow or download *Why We Sleep* by Matthew Walker and *Life Time: The New Science of the Body Clock* by Russell Foster, whose expert advice I will be calling on later in this chapter.

Late nights, air travel, work, having babies, IVF treatment and breast cancer have all taken their toll on my sleep miles. Here, I'm going to talk you through the basics and explain how I managed to take control of my nights after decades of sleep abuse, and how introducing new daily walking habits and 'nature snacks' helped me recover.

Now the huge importance of sleep has been recognised, I could speculate that my bad sleep history played a role in my breast cancer. Professor Russell Foster confirms the link, although I think the really deep dive that's needed there is for a different book. Instead, let's explore what we can all do to improve things and achieve what's called good 'sleep hygiene'. How do you scrub up for a good night in an easy and affordable way?

 Travel

I remember coming home from filming a travel show in South Africa. I got on a jam-packed flight, found I was in a middle seat and thought, 'Ugh, I'm, not going to get any sleep at all.' Then I went out like a light and stayed that way until wheels-down in London. It was the best flight of my life in terms of sleep – but mostly it's not like that, is it? Travel often means a night out of bed and a sleep deficit. So, too, does child rearing and any sad or bad situation that is consuming your thoughts. Or maybe you were just the last one standing in a great bar with your mates? Whatever the reason, you are probably not getting enough time in your own sleep temple.

The truth about jet lag

Jet lag is nothing to do with distance and time. It's to do with your circadian system and it impacts everyone – and I mean everyone, even the heir to the throne.

Professor Russell Foster tells me, 'You don't feel ghastly moving from London to, let's say, New York, simply because you've shifted five hours on the clock – it is because all your internal systems have ceased to be aligned with respect to one another. When I got my CBE from Prince William, he asked what he could do about jet lag. I responded: "Well, sir, the good news is we know what causes it, a protein, and what's more, we can cure it." Then I told him that so far, this was only in mice. "We're still working on humans."'

Your body clock

Humans need natural light from dawn onwards. This is partly because the quest for sleep starts the second you wake up. Circadian systems are critical. They are our body clocks, an internal representation of the biological day, if you will. For these systems to work optimally, we need our body's day to be set to the real day, and to do that, we need exposure to the light–dark cycle, particularly the morning light.

Since learning about circadian systems, I've learned to worship The Morning Light. I'm giving it capitals because it deserves That Much Respect.

Morning light is crucial because it readies our bodies for the twenty-four hours to come. Put simply, the light at sunrise is key, because this is when the sun starts to splay out its colours, and these early colours interact and go to work on the human brain. We soak up that light through our eyes (those rods and cones you learned about in your school biology lessons), and there's also a newly discovered third photoreceptor that interacts with the 'master clock' in the brain – the suprachiasmatic nucleus (SCN) – sending a message to every cell telling it to get ready for the tasks that lie ahead. It's a direct connection between light and brain and body; it's the pathway that sets our circadian timing and regulates most of our circadian rhythms.

As you may be aware, serotonin has multiple functions: it influences learning and memory, creates happiness, and regulates our body temperature, sleep, sexual behaviour and hunger. A lack of serotonin is thought to play a role in depression, anxiety, mania and other mental health conditions. So, quite important.

Most serotonin is produced in the gut (although ten per cent is produced in the brain), but you might not know that every living cell on the planet, including bacteria found in the gut, releases ultraviolet light. This UV light is liberated at key times during the day, synched to your circadian clock. If your circadian rhythm is fully functional, that morning light tells your brain what time it is, your brain passes the message on to your gut bacteria, and they release a burst of ultraviolet light to make serotonin for you. Magic.

The sun directs the colours of the rainbow at us all day long, and beyond that spectrum are infrared and ultraviolet light. Every colour does something for our bodies. After the sun reaches its highest point in the sky, it starts to systematically take them away. (Take note: there is no blue light – the light given off by our ubiquitous screens – before sunrise or after sunset.)

To optimise human function, we should try to get out into these rainbow colours in the same, certain, predictable way every day. Sadly, most of us now live an indoor life, illuminated by bulbs and gazing at screens. Artificial lights are foreign to our brains because they don't, as a rule, contain every colour of the rainbow (they definitely don't contain ultraviolet or infrared), and they never change.

The electric light above your head illuminating the pages of this book, or the very screen you might be reading it on, gives your eyes the same colour message all day long, when what your brain really wants is variation. In other words, what it wants, what it needs, is NATURAL LIGHT.

All of which is to say that morning light is an important part of helping you get set for the night ahead. This is why I stick my head out of the bathroom window as soon as I wake up, rain or shine, right after my morning wee. First thing in the morning is the traditional time for 'tea + pee', so now please make it 'tea + pee + daylight'.

Only this morning, I pulled my waterproofs on top of my PJs and sat yogi-like in the window to catch my lux (the measurement of light), listening to the meditative tap of raindrops on Gore-Tex. The light is obviously lower during winter and on cloudy days, so I up my exposure from ten or fifteen minutes to twenty minutes. I occasionally have to get up earlier to build this into my day, but I make every minute matter by combining it with breathwork to prepare myself for the day ahead (see Chapter 5).

I accept it can feel tricky, impossible even, to *make* time to sit in natural light. I didn't do it until I was diagnosed with breast cancer and contemplated my own mortality. I finally understood I wasn't indestructible as I had previously imagined, and that I had to do everything I could to support my health. Sleep is a huge part of that. I will do anything to help me sleep better, and if that means sitting in an anorak with my face half out of my bathroom window every morning, that's fine. It's not glamorous or cool. But it's fine.

The morning light and its capacity to set my internal clocks to the external world – nudging them forward so I tune in to the sleep–wake cycle – has been a life changer for me. Science might eventually tell me it was a lifesaver. Even on days when I'm tired and feeling lazy, I do my morning light routine and then, if I want to go back to bed for Sunday cuddles with my children, or to read, or watch a movie – I do. The key, as with everything else in this book, is routine and good habits. The only time I break my sleep routine is if I feel the need for an afternoon nap. I feel zero guilt about that. I regard myself as being in recovery from breast cancer, and I always will. Plus, I'm part Greek. Greeks are big on napping. It's my heritage!

The dawn phenomenon

There's something you should know about waking up. The risk of having a stroke or heart attack is significantly higher in the morning, and that's because the biological switch from the sleep-resting state to the active state is preparing us for a day of action: hunting, gathering and moving camps – or doing the school run, heading to the office and sifting through hundreds of emails. Our internal clocks anticipate our increased activity, our blood pressure goes up, cortisol and glucose levels rise and our blood platelet count increases (presumably in anticipation of an increased risk of damage and therefore the need to clot).

This is called the dawn phenomenon: a combination of natural changes and reactions in the body that happen while you're asleep but preparing to wake. If you're healthy, this is a wonderful, adaptive response that means you can get up, get out and go on with your day. If you're not so healthy, this surge in blood pressure and stress hormones, and the increased stickiness of your blood, makes you more likely to have a heart attack or a stroke. If you're reading this chapter between 6am and midday, beware, because that's the time we're at most risk! Getting good sleep will help protect you from this. Mother Nature, as usual, knows best.

Improving your sleep hygiene

Without a doubt, learning to expose myself to the morning light and setting my internal clock to the external world for the next twenty-four hours is the best thing I have done in my quest for quality sleep. I suggest you try it too.

Here are some other things that can affect your sleep:

An evening stroll

I avoid vigorous exercise just before bedtime. A gentle walk is perfect, but anything strenuous that increases your core body temperature is a hindrance. A drop in core body temperature has been associated with better sleep quality, so while exercising before bedtime may not be inherently harmful, a sweaty evening workout can affect sleep efficiency. You need a polite promenade somewhere instead.

And it's not just about the physical aspect of walking – is it ever? What you need to do is to 'walk off' your day. It's really important to step back and do something that detaches you from the day's events – because, as Professor Russell Foster says, 'The main enemy of sleep is stress.'

I know that many of us are leading incredibly stressful lives. We are being nudged, pushed and full-on shoved ever forwards by technology, competing deadlines, stroppy bosses and demanding children (feel free to add your own issues to that list). Everyone's stresses will be different, but there is one universal rule: in order to get a restful, restorative night's sleep, you have to let them all go as night comes. We know that walking helps us process thoughts, so walking alone, or with a friend or relative, can be a placid way to unwind and soothe the mind.

Professor Shane O'Mara of Trinity College in Dublin, a neuroscientist and passionate advocate of walking, believes that in terms of calming us down and cheering us up, we can't walk too much! An evening stroll helps you 'set the intention' of going to sleep. Think of it as unplugging. You only need twenty or thirty minutes – and please don't spend them looking for conclusions. When you sleep deeply, your brain comes up with solutions to problems; it thinks while you are offline. Let the motion of your body and the rhythm of a walk set the course to a place where this can happen.

Cool it

The Mediterranean part of me loves heat and sunshine but I have now retrained myself to sleep with my windows open to keep the bedroom cool. The metabolism establishes a target temperature for the body, and if we are warmer or colder than it likes, the body will regulate itself. Body temperature naturally lowers when we're going to sleep, so it makes sense to sleep in a cooler room, giving the body's thermostat less work to do.[2]

Meals and munchies

Similarly, don't put your digestive system into overdrive in the evening either. When you can, it makes sense to eat your bigger meals earlier in the day, by having a substantial brekky and lunch, and then a smaller portion in the evening. If I'm out with friends or family, I may still be eating at 9pm, but most nights now I'm done by 6pm or 7pm, and I resist the urge to snack on the sofa. You want a rule for this? Keep food light at night!

Full of beans

Avoid excessive consumption of caffeine. Coffee is so ubiquitous, it's easy to forget it's a drug. Actually, it's the most widely used psychoactive stimulant in the world. We don't really understand how caffeine works, but we do know it is structurally similar to adenosine, a neurotransmitter in the brain that makes us sleepy. When we drink coffee it binds to and blocks our adenosine receptors. When adenosine binds to these receptors it causes drowsiness by slowing down our nerve cell activity. Coffee blocks this reaction and disrupts the nervous system's monitoring of adenosine, allowing the other neurotransmitters, dopamine and glutamate, the brain's home-grown stimulants, the freedom to do their thing. In other words, coffee prevents adenosine from slowing down our neural activity, making us feel more alert and awake. If you drink caffeine regularly, the brain's chemistry changes over time, and brain cells begin to grow *more* adenosine receptors, which is how caffeine tolerance develops. Because the brain has more adenosine receptors, it takes more caffeine to block a significant proportion of them and achieve the same desired effect . . . you can see where this is going.

Caffeine has a half-life of six hours and a quarter-life of twelve hours, so if you have a coffee at midday, a quarter of that caffeine will still be circulating in your brain at midnight.

I used to drink coffee all day, stuck in a cycle you may recognise in yourself. I didn't see it then, but I do now. If you're fuelling your waking day with lots and lots of caffeine, it means you're wired when you need to go to sleep, and there's a tendency to reverse this stimulation with sedation. Here comes that big glass of wine or a bottle of beer to help us 'wind down'. If this is you, then you're in something called a stimulant/sedative feedback loop. It's really important to appreciate that alcohol *is a sedative* and interferes with your night-time brain activity (like memory formation, toxin-scrubbing and all the rest of the stuff you really, really need), so if you're serious about sleeping more and better, you have to escape the loop.

Personally, I no longer have coffee after midday, and when I do have one, it's a half-shot with lots of frothy plant-based milk.

Electric dreams

Electricity has changed the world. It has fuelled our industrial and digital revolutions, but it hasn't necessarily done us humans a favour. We are no longer connected to Earth's day–night cycle. We don't fall asleep in the evening or when the candles run out. Our houses look like Christmas trees with lights a-blazing for most of the day. To get your body more in tune with the real-world light cycle (and help you get to sleep), keep your levels of light low in the evening. Avoid brightly lit rooms, including that incredibly well-illuminated bathroom mirror you stare into while cleaning your teeth, and invest in some dimmers or adjustable clip-on lamps for the bedroom.

If your house is more 'high season Las Vegas' than 'cosy candlelit cottage' at night, it will increase your alertness and push your body clock forward. Then, my friend, it will be your turn to sit with your face stuck out of the bathroom window, trying to regulate your circadian rhythms.

Screen test

The blue light our screens emit has vexed sleep scientists since our love affair with technology began. As I explained on page 95, there is no blue light before sunrise or after sunset in the natural world, and our modern near-constant exposure to it wreaks havoc on our cellular clocks. If you're gazing like a ring-tailed lemur into your phone deep into the night, your body thinks it's daytime, and all those lovely 'repair' functions get thrown out of whack.

Professor Russell Foster uses the analogy of an orchestra to explain this. He says: 'You've got this master clock, the conductor, ticking away, and all the musicians playing with reference to the conductor. If you shoot the conductor, the musicians start to play at a slightly different time and you end up with a cacophony when we should be in harmony.'

When it comes to screens (including the football-pitch-sized TVs most people seem to have these days) there's another issue: the interaction and stimulation.

Doom-scrolling on your phone or devouring a highly charged television series in bed at night is going to keep you awake. Your brain will demand to know what comes next. The same goes for social media, which uses a cerebral reward system similar to that of computer games and electronic gambling apps. It's all about the dopamine hit of views and likes and refreshes, which keeps you coming back for more. And more. And more. That's their genius. These apps and devices are designed to increase our appetite for them, so at night, put your phones and your gadgets away in a drawer. Make a plan to ignore any incoming traffic and stick to it. And turn off your TV.

Immediately before bed adopt behaviours that relax you instead. Read a favourite book, listen to music, knit (this works for Michelle Obama) – whatever activity you find soothing. Another tip comes from Allison Harvey, a professor of clinical psychology and director of the beautifully named Golden Bear Sleep and Mood Research Clinic at the University of California, Berkeley. She recommends removing all clock faces from your bedroom. This has really improved things for me. What good does it do, knowing it's 2.35am if you haven't been able to drop off, or if you wake up long before you're supposed to? It only triggers more anxiety.

Dealing with wakefulness

If you do wake up in the night, though, it isn't the end of the world. It's natural. In the pre-Industrial era, people went to bed at 9pm or 10pm and then got up again at midnight. But they weren't anguished insomniacs. They were pottering about with their children, perhaps having a meal (although I wouldn't recommend that, as we discussed in the last chapter – it will just get the body digesting again), maybe throwing wood on their fire. Then they'd just . . . go back to sleep. The twenty-first century is built to handle monophasic sleepers (people who sleep in a single stretch) but many humans are bi-phasic (sleeping in two stretches) or multi-phasic (sleeping in several stretches). Lots of mammals are the same, as well as birds and insects.[3]

So, if you do wake up in the night, try not to worry about it. Lie in bed for a few minutes, telling yourself you're resting. Maybe try some breathwork or meditation. I sometimes find a really boring podcast to listen to – I usually have one ready to go. I like someone with a low-pitched voice talking about something I'm not particularly interested in – like cricket. Works a treat – I can't even remember how boring it was the following morning!

If you can't get back to sleep after ten minutes, then get up and go to a different room, and read a chapter of a loved book under a low light or listen to soft music. Head back to bed only when you feel sleepy again.

Avoid tech-induced anxiety

I'm making this a separate section because this is a different issue to busying your brain with screentime when you should be going to sleep.

Anticipatory anxiety is the fear of things we can't predict or control happening at some future point. If your brain knows there's going to be an onslaught of information first thing – for example, when you check the phone that you have left on your bedside table – then, Professor Matthew Walker argues, it lightens your sleep throughout the night. Think about those times when you go to bed knowing you have to get up early for an appointment or a train or a flight. I don't know about you, but I never sleep as well on those nights. They're an example of anticipatory anxiety for me.

To avoid it, keep all of your technology outside the bedroom; don't look at it last thing at night, and try not to make it the first thing you do in the morning either. Get yourself into the morning light and have a cup of warm lemon water to awaken the body instead. Having your phone in the bedroom also causes sleep procrastination – a delay in going to sleep that reduces your total sleep time (we call it 'fannying around' in our house). Checking online orders/emails/messages/Instagram at 10pm *isn't* going to save you a few minutes the next day – it's just going to eat into your precious night.

Matthew Walker's book has the BEST tip for dealing with this. I love it and I want to share it with you. If you're absolutely wedded to keeping your phone in the bedroom, make it a rule that you can only use it standing up. Once you're tired of doing that, you've got to turn it to airplane mode and put it away.

Don't look at the light too blue

Recently I've started wearing blue-light blocking glasses in the evening, if I'm working a bit late at the laptop or the house lights are too bright (I skulk around the house turning them all down or off!). I think blue-light blocking glasses are a modern necessity because of the massive intrusion of artificial light in our lives. Good ones should absorb the harmful wavelengths of light to help protect us. I've given them to my children too, for their night time reading to help wind them down, and, so far, they're working a treat for all of us.

Cocoon with a view

Make your bedroom a haven for sleep. Get some beautiful house plants and try using a diffuser with essential oils – you can make one with bamboo skewers and a jam jar, it doesn't have to be from an expensive homeware shop. Seek out good sheets and bed clothing, the best you can afford. We spend more than thirty per cent of our time in bed, so a good mattress and pillows, and pleasant surroundings, are an investment in your sleep, which is an investment in your health. If you're travelling, take some of your bedtime goodies with you. It's not a luxury; it's about familiarity and the ease it gives your senses.

Sleep-reading wearable tech doesn't necessarily need a place in this new cocoon of yours. These tools are good at telling you how long you've slept (which is different to how long you've been in bed), but they're not reliable for much else.[4] Honestly, the best measure of how you've slept is *you*. How do you feel in the morning? How are you managing throughout the day? Is your family giving you a wide berth because you're so grumpy? You know yourself better than any app, and the answer to a bout of insomnia might be more analogue than digital. You might just need to restyle your bedroom a bit.

Snoring

Some things get worse as we get older – snoring is one of them. Taking a pragmatic, unemotional approach to a partner's snoring is essential. Ear plugs are option one. Finding an alternative sleeping place is option two, and should be taken seriously. It's no reflection on the nature of your relationship with your partner; it just means both of you will get a better night's sleep. Snoring has a comedic value – how often do we see it in a funny film or hear it as the punchline to a gag? But it's not really funny. It's disruptive, destructive, even. One of you can't sleep, the other one is anxious about keeping their beloved awake. That's not conducive to a good night for either of you.

Heavy snoring may be an indicator of something more serious: a condition called obstructive sleep apnoea. This can raise the risk for diabetes, obesity, hypertension, stroke, heart attack and other cardiovascular problems. Snoring is caused by the tongue not having enough room in the back of the throat; oxygen levels drop and hormones such as cortisone and adrenaline surge, which can contribute to high blood pressure and irregularities of the heart.

Building a sleep routine

If I have one overarching rule for myself, it's this: I stick to the sleep routine I've created for myself, even at weekends. Obviously, I fall off the wagon occasionally, when I'm travelling for work or have a birthday celebration or an unexpected late night with friends (socialising and bonds are very important to our overall health, too) but the rule for me now is a regular sleep routine.

I met the British astronaut Tim Peake while writing this book, and he admitted that he'd kept a strict sleep timetable during his six months on board the international space station . . . until he flew over the Bahamas one bedtime. The flash of Caribbean blue through the porthole was mesmeric, he said, and he rushed to get his camera to record it. But, of course, he was looking at a thrillingly bright light and waking himself up at the exact time he should have been winding down. 'When I got into my sleeping bag and closed my eyes,' he confided, 'nothing happened, absolutely nothing.'

It may sound boring, but we all respond well to routine in certain areas of life, and sleep is one of them. This is another good use for the eighty/twenty rule, which I mentioned on page 60. For eighty per cent of the time, I stick to my sleep routine; the other twenty per cent, things go the way they go.

Why you have to stick to it

I didn't take sleep or stress seriously until later in life. I can't know for sure if it made me more vulnerable to breast cancer – there's no medical test for that. But, with hindsight, I know I lived a life that wore me out, and I fear that my body was less resilient because of it. There is evidence that the disrupted sleeping patterns that arise from long periods of shift work can contribute to breast, prostate and colorectal cancer.

Sleep deprivation is particularly significant in the Western world[5] and can affect around one in three of us at any time. However, we each have the capacity to change this, with thought, acceptance and commitment. I did. I had to pick apart my day and my habits, my very idea of myself as an owl, to make this systemic change, but I am glad I did, because my sleep is much more ordered now.

You might think, 'Oh, I haven't got *time* to do all that. And I don't need to; I'm managing fine on four/five hours a night.'

Cancer survivors like me, and people who have been through other major illnesses and breakdowns, understand the old adage that if you don't make time for your health, you will be forced to make time for your illness.

I asked Professor Russell Foster what he thought about skating by on less sleep than you need, and he could not have been clearer.

'It's just not worth juggling with knives, Julia,' he said. 'You might get away with it; chances are, you're going to lose.'

A conversation with Professor Russell Foster

I spoke to Russell in the library at his home. He looked every inch the Oxford don, but he's far from a tweedy, ivory-tower academic. He cheerfully admits he's an owl rather than a lark, and he's very glad that he's a professor and can schedule his meetings from 10am instead of 8am. On the odd occasion he can't sleep, he tunes in to Radio 4 Extra, and he's unafraid to say that bedrooms should be havens for sleep and sex, adding that the British can be real penny-pinchers when it comes to investing in a decent goose-down duvet.

'We get a bit cheesy about spending money on sleep,' he says with a smile – though he's making a serious point, because he knows more than pretty much anyone else in the world how crucial it is for us.

I begin with the most fundamental question of all.

Why do we sleep?

Russell: For me, there is no magic. Sleep is a period of physical inactivity during which time we do essential biology. When we are active, we're getting out there finding food, finding mates, taking in lots and lots of information, which we can't process online very easily. So, you take it offline and then you can start to lay down memory, to problem-solve. And, since you have built up a whole bunch of toxins as a result of metabolic activity during the day, you deal with them at the same time.

And what happens if you don't?

Russell: You see fluctuations in mood. If you have a tired brain, it is more likely to remember negative experiences than positive ones. You tend to be more impulsive, take risks, use stimulants and then sedatives to reverse their effects. Your cognition goes, your memory goes, your communication skills start to break down, and you lose social connectivity.

[Interestingly, the professor points to the 1980s culture when 'pulling an all-nighter' was a badge of honour.]

Russell: The ramifications of that were really serious. If you want [an example of] people who lack empathy, who don't listen to others, are more prone to risk-taking and impulsivity, then look at the chronically sleep-deprived eighties. You got a global financial crisis because you had people who were wired, doing incredibly important jobs, not objectively able to assess any given situation accurately, because of their lack of sleep.

Lack of sleep also makes humans prone to micro-sleeps, where we fall asleep without warning for a few seconds. They're very dangerous if someone is driving or operating machinery. Interestingly, we often don't even know we've had one, believing ourselves to have remained awake, as normal.

Then we grade through into increased levels of cardiovascular disease, reduced immunity to infection, type 2 diabetes, and higher rates of cancer. The World Health Organization has now classified night-shift work as a probable carcinogen because the data is so clear. It's really serious.

We may be the only species in the world which is able to override biology, staying awake when our brains and bodies are saying we should be asleep. But if you operate that way, it's like having an engine stuck in first gear. You have wonderful acceleration – our fight-or-flight mechanism – but if you keep any engine permanently in first, you destroy it. Lack of sleep is so much more than feeling tired at an inconvenient time. It has both short-term and long-term health impacts.

In just one night of no sleep, you can actually measure increased levels of beta-amyloid deposition within the brain and high levels in the cerebral spinal fluid. *[Beta amyloid is the toxic protein I mentioned on page 92.]* I don't think you would say that poor sleep is going to cause dementia, but what we know now is that poor sleep in the middle years is a risk factor for the development of dementia in later years. It could be because there's a critical threshold where you've deposited all this garbage within the brain, but not taken your need to sleep seriously enough to clear it out.'

[And unlike gut health, which can be hugely improved within a fortnight, as Professor Tim Spector told us in Chapter 3, you cannot reverse this process. That's why you need to get to work on your sleep today.]

Is it true that driving while sleepy can be more dangerous than driving drunk?

Russell: Alertness peaks in adults at around 11am to 12pm, and then slides down to a low point at around about 5am or 6am. A study in Australia compared the drop in our cognitive performance across the day to what happens with alcohol consumption. In this study, the dropping in our cognitive performance at 4am or 5am was minus-twenty. But the drop when we were legally drunk was minus-fifteen. So, our ability to drive a car at 4am was worse than if we [were to] consume sufficient alcohol to make us legally drunk. I say to people, 'Don't do it!' How many of us have got into a people carrier and driven off early to get an extra day on the beach for the children when we are on holiday? We shouldn't be doing that!

Is there any good news?

Russell: [Sleep is] amazingly dynamic, and if you are at a party which finishes later than 10pm, then so be it! *[He's chuckling here, and clearly supports my eighty/twenty rule. He's also adamant different people have different needs. You simply cannot take a sleep average and impose it on everybody. It's like shoe size; it would be absurd to make everybody wear the same size shoe. Three things contribute to our individual sleep patterns: genetics, age and exposure to light. When it comes to our genetic inheritance, as Russell puts it, 'Our parents are still telling us when to get up and go to bed!' As for age, by the time you are in your late fifties or early sixties, you'll be wanting to get up and go to bed at the same times as when you were ten. Finally, it's about where and when you see light, which is where getting your circadian systems in synch can help.]*

Russell: There's too much screaming by the sergeant majors of sleep that you must do this, and you must do that. You want some structure, but not for it to be so terrifying that you get anxious. If you feel as if you are performing optimally during the day, that's a good indicator. If an alarm clock drives you out of bed in the week and you oversleep at the weekend, that's not. Really, most people don't have a sleep problem; they have a stress or an anxiety problem.

[Of course, that anxiety can come from fretting about insomnia. Unbelievably, Russell was once asked for help by a man who set his alarm for 3am so he could check his sleep monitor to see how much sleep he'd had. Afterwards, he couldn't drop off again. It hadn't occurred to him it was this obsessive monitoring of his sleep that was making him sleepless. It's an amusing anecdote, but indicative of how troubled we are as a society. I mean, why not just . . . carry on sleeping?!

Russell believes we would all feel more relaxed about sleep if we accepted that we usually wake up several times a night without really 'coming to', and that even if we do awaken, we will nod off again.]

Russell: I think it's such an important point, because people don't know that's the default position for humans and therefore they get very anxious if they do wake up, assuming they're not going to fall back to sleep. If all you manage is another fifteen or twenty minutes, that's still worth having.'

And how does walking help?

Russell: We've got this master clock in the brain which coordinates the billions and billions of individual cellular clocks organised throughout the organ system. Walking – any physical exercise – will help set the clock, which then stabilises the sleep–wake cycle. The dream combination is going out for a walk in the morning, which gives you light exposure and exercise at the same time. All these things are profoundly affective and will improve mood and motivation, which is the key to developing a regular exercise programme. Once you start, you will find it easier to keep going.

[Earlier I mentioned how a walk in the evening is a great way to de-stress. Russell is talking about a walk to wake your body up for the day and expose yourself to light. These walks achieve two different things and, of course, I approve because the more walking the better in my book.]

What's next for sleep?

Russell: In the nineteenth century, a candle cost a penny, a working man's entire daily wage, so of course sleep was determined by the light–dark cycle and changed with the seasons. Then we developed cheap electric light and essentially, we invaded the night. We threw away sleep without realising the importance of this aspect of our biology.

Now we are looking ahead to a time when medicine could be prescribed according to circadian rhythms, or even when a twenty-four-hour-a-day workforce is hired by chronotype – that is, whether they are larks or owls.

Humans need six hours of sleep in every twenty-four hours as a bare minimum. People are brilliant at deluding themselves that they're OK even when they're driving their waking day with coffee and a single-minded, overwhelming desire to do what they need to do. We, as a species, can do that but there are long-term consequences for individuals and for society. We're not going to put 24/7 living back in the bottle, but we are starting to ask how to mitigate some of the problems it causes.

Shiftwork, sleep and cancer

In researching my own breast cancer, I came across the work done in June 2019 by scientists from sixteen different countries at the International Agency for Research on Cancer in Lyon, France. They were looking at what happens to humans when our normal circadian rhythms are interrupted by working night shifts for extended periods – there's a huge nocturnal workforce in the healthcare, manufacturing, transport, retail and services sectors.

What they found was truly terrifying. They concluded that disrupted sleeping patterns are 'probably carcinogenic to humans'.[6] A subsequent report in the *Lancet* in August that year was of particular interest to me. It detailed a raised risk of breast cancer among night-shift nurses, based on a control group of 6,000 cases from five different countries.[7] I'm not a nurse, but I have done my fair share of night shifts in the broadcasting industry, with its twenty-four-hour-a-day demands and urgent deadlines. Now do you see why I ask myself how much damage I unknowingly did to my body?

I asked Russell outright what he thought about this.

'I would say that, if you're vulnerable, poor sleep is an increased risk factor,' he said. 'I would never say it would cause cancer, but if you're on that spectrum, then it can nudge you over.'

If you are currently doing night shifts here are a few things Russell and his team suggest to mitigate the impact. If possible, limit night-shift work to three or four years on and three or four years off. Be mindful of what you eat, reduce a high-fat, high-sugar diet and replace with small protein rich and easy to digest meals and snacks. See if it is possible for your employer to introduce bright light stations to increase alertness, and make sure that you get frequent health checks to help detect problems before they become chronic conditions. Finally, when you do manage to sleep, pay attention to ALL the earlier tips about making your bedroom a cocoon with blackout blinds and by wearing an eye mask. Your eyelids are so thin that trying to sleep without a mask will mean some light penetrating and impacting the quality of your sleep.

The upside of downtime

I don't want to make you feel gloomy, so let's think about the positives. Albert Einstein enjoyed a good ten hours of sleep a night. Top sports stars such as Roger Federer do, too. Sleep won't make you a mini-Einstein or a Grand Slam tennis star, but it will make you better at everything you do.

I love my bed these days. Even in adulthood, it gives me a childlike delight. I remember once as a little girl visiting my grandmother – my *yiyi* – in Greece, and resisting the Greek tradition of an afternoon nap. It was all too exciting to want to miss a minute of the day. My dad started tickling my back and we were laughing and joking together – and that's the last thing I remember until I woke up two hours later. I often think back to

Sleep Chart*

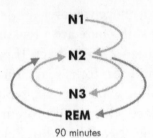

90 minutes

We know that sleep is not a passive process and we experience complex changes in brain activity. An EEG (electroencephalogram) gives us an insight into the brain's electrical activity when we sleep. There are four STAGES of sleep that everyone goes through several times each night. These are made up of two TYPES of sleep: REM (rapid eye movement) and Non-REM.

When you first fall asleep you enter Non-REM sleep which is made up of three stages, each becoming progressively deeper. This is the restful and restorative sleep where your body is being repaired.

Did You Know?

Non-REM sleep lowers
muscle tone,
body temperature,
heart rate
and blood pressure

Stage N1 is where you experience light sleep. This is when you are nodding off but can be easily woken by a slight sound or movement. It is often considered a state of transition between wakefulness and sleep.

Stage N2 is still a light sleep but slightly deeper than Stage N1. If left undisturbed, you continue to Stage N3.

Stage N3 (also called slow wave or deep sleep) is when you are in a deep sleep, are less responsive to noises and activity in your envirionment and may find it difficult to awaken. Some of you may feel disorientated if woken from this stage of sleep.

REM (rapid eye movement), the fourth stage of sleep, is where the body switches off and the brain receives extra blood and processes the day's events. This sleep consolidates learning and helps develop social and emotional abilities. In REM sleep you dream, and during this period of sleep your body is deeply relaxed.

Each cycle lasts around 90 minutes and a good night's sleep usually consists of five cycles, whereas disturbed sleep consists of lots of shortened or incomplete cycles. REM sleep increases with each cycle and Stage N3 sleep decreases.

* This chart has been specially created for *Walk Yourself Happy* by The Sleep Charity www.thesleepcharity.org.uk. Further information is available in *Understanding Your Sleep*, an ebook written by Lisa Artis, deputy CEO, The Sleep Charity.

that scene, because it's such a happy sleep memory, guaranteed to make me nod off.

I reached for it and replayed it many times when I was first diagnosed with cancer and then during my treatment. I had bouts of insomnia in the weeks before my mastectomy, waking in the middle of the night, scared, and then facing a day of fatigue and moodiness. Learning to prioritise sleep has helped my recovery. I prepare for it in all the ways I have just described, and cherish those rituals rather than seeing them as an imposition. These days, I go to sleep early and rarely need an alarm to wake up. If I am still asleep when my alarm goes off, I find it very . . . alarming! It took me a little time to get here, and it will for you too, but you can do it.

The most inactive creature in the world is probably the three-toed sloth, which sleeps around nineteen hours out of every twenty-four. What can I say? Be more sloth.

Happy camping

As the former president of the Camping and Caravanning Club, I know first-hand the benefits of sleeping 'outside' – and I am a big fan. It is something I do with my kids at least once a year, so they understand the ebb and flow of a night outdoors. They love camping: that sense of agency, of independence, of being on their own in a tent (while, of course, I'm only an inch away, listening to every giggle and every marshmallow being stuffed in). They sleep brilliantly outdoors, whether it's under canvas or in a caravan, because they are (usually) properly tired by the end of the day, it's dark and there's much less to disturb them. In short, they have tuned in to their natural surroundings.

The same principles apply to us, the grown-ups. Post-Covid, I went on a three-day mindfulness retreat in the blissful surroundings of Sharpham House overlooking the River Dart in Devon. It's a Grade-1 listed Georgian mansion, but you don't sleep in it, you sleep in bell tents, embedded in nature, in the gardens. It's a little bit of heaven on Earth.

You are encouraged to stay off your phones (no scrolling and posting) and away from alcohol, and instead to get stuck into physical activities such as kayaking on the Dart, as well as embracing walking, meditation and mindfulness. Dinner is a veggie meal, and it's bed by 10pm, latest. In the morning there's fifteen minutes of silence – no chatter, just nodding and smiling, so you get to hear the sounds of the day, the trees whispering and the birds singing. (I loved this, though it made me realise I would find a silent retreat really difficult, no matter how much my family might want me to go on one!)

I had some of the best nights' sleep of my life at Sharpham House. It confirmed everything I've been banging on about as president of the Camping and Caravanning Club – that sleeping outside helps reset your circadian rhythms.

As little as one weekend filled with natural light and true darkness is enough to work this magic, according to research done by a team from Boulder University in Colorado, who sent volunteers into the wilderness in summer and winter and tracked how fast their circadian rhythms realigned to the seasons.[8]

I have slept on the banks of the Thames in a caravan, I have bivouacked among volcanoes in Iceland and snoozed freestyle under a hedge in Berkshire. Wherever you are, these benefits are universal.

PS: Recent research has shown that ninety-eight per cent of campers take part in outdoor activities . . . like walking.[9]

Sue's seeds of wisdom: A walking visualisation exercise to improve sleep

Whether you are habitually a good sleeper or someone who regularly struggles with sleep, almost everyone experiences insomnia at some point in their lives.

We all have times when events overwhelm us and worries keep us awake; our minds can feel like washing machines with thoughts going round and round in a never-ending cycle. The knack of switching off eludes us, and the longer it goes on, the more anxious we become about not getting enough sleep.

The trick to turning off an overactive mind in this situation is to shift your attention and occupy it with something else.

Visualisation is a tried-and-tested technique for doing this.

For this exercise, you need to enlist your mind's eye to recreate a place in which you have felt relaxed and peaceful.

Rather than being stationary, imagine you are moving through it. For example, you might be strolling along a favourite beach with the lapping and crashing of waves, or hiking along a ridge with panoramic views of the landscape below, or walking through a bluebell-filled wood with shafts of light streaming through the trees.

These are my favourites. You will have yours.

As you progress along your chosen route, shift your focus and take in as many sensory details as you can, including the temperature of the air on your skin, the colour of the sky and the shapes of the clouds, the various sounds of nature around you and the details of the plants and trees.

You might be on your own or you might be accompanied by your dog or by someone you love. The important thing is for you to feel you are safe.

Keep going and find your rhythm as you would on an actual walk. Focus on your breathing and the sensation of the ground under your feet.

It may take a while, but all you need to do is stay on your chosen route and you will reach the elusive destination of sleep.

5

Walking, Breathing, Living

'We live most life, whoever breathes most air.'
Elizabeth Barrett Browning, 'Love'

You might have noticed I have a big nose. Someone once joked that it casts its own shadow. I'm proud of it and wear it with pride, as I was encouraged to do from an early age by my Mama Mou Chrissi. It gives me character, apparently, and it's quite Greek-looking, which I don't mind, but it turns out I've been using it incorrectly for a long time.

Rather, I haven't been using it enough – which is a shame for a vessel of this size.

You would be forgiven for thinking you already know how to breathe. You're doing it right now. You just open your mouth and suck in air, right?

Apparently not.

Even though we breathe unconsciously, most of us make these three common mistakes:

- we breathe into the chest and upper body
- we breathe through the mouth (known as chronic mouth-breathing)
- we breathe too much

Learning to breathe properly can be life-changing and can have a profound impact on our health and well-being. Beyond its primary function, our nasal cycle (which sees us unconsciously make one nostril dominant over the other every couple of hours) is linked to higher-order brain processes and other major bodily systems: neuroendocrine, cardiovascular, fuel-regulatory, immune and gastrointestinal.[1] The humble nose is responsible for about thirty functions within the human body – who knew?

The power of breath has been shared down the centuries and across cultures. Needless to say, we've mislaid it somewhere in modern life, along with its cornucopia of benefits. My big sister Gina is no pulmonaut (someone who has stumbled upon the powers of breathing), but it turns out she has struck an accidental chord with her WhatsApp handle, which says: 'Inhale the future, exhale the past.' So, let's start from there.

Breathing well – which means through your nose and not through your mouth – boosts your immune system and your circulation, as well as perking up your mood and even your sexual functioning. It also triggers the sinuses to release nitric oxide, a molecule that plays an essential role in delivering oxygen to our cells – we can absorb eighteen per cent more oxygen breathing nasally than we do breathing orally.

On average, we breathe in and out 25,000 times a day without thinking about it, but often those breaths are the oxygenated equivalent of a late-night kebab: they'll get you home, but they have little nutritional value and won't make you feel that great. This chapter is designed to ensure your 25,000 breaths nourish you instead. The great thing is that you don't have to do your breathwork at home. There are plenty of breathing exercises that you can do while you are walking – on page 148, you'll find one that can improve your 'breathing fitness' and your physical fitness at the same time.

Understanding your breath

Now I'm going to give you a little test that can help predict the future. Be warned: this could scare you! It's all to do with lung capacity, which decreases as we get older, and is a broad predictor of our longevity and overall health. The tests are taken from the work of Anders Olsson, a passionate pulmonaut and author of the book *Conscious Breathing*.

Your ability to hold your breath increases the more you relax, which is why you should try not to think of these tests as *tests*. Try thinking of them as relaxation exercises instead. Keep your mouth closed and breathe through your nose for both.

Test one

- First, sit down with your back straight, and relax for a couple of minutes (when was the last time you did that?).
- Take a small breath in and a small one out *through your nose*, roughly two to three seconds each way. After you have exhaled (softly), hold your nose and start a timer. Keep your mouth closed.
- Let go of your nose and inhale again (through your nose) *as soon* as you feel the urge to breathe. The in-breath through the nose should be as gentle as the breath before your nose-hold. If this inhale is forceful, then sorry – you've held your breath for too long and you won't get a true reading. Be honest with yourself; it's not a competition against anyone else.

Test two

- I'd suggest you do the second test at another time during the day. Sit down with your back straight and relax for a couple of minutes (you're welcome).

- Stand up and take the same small breath in and out through the nostrils (mouth closed) for two to three seconds on the inhale, and the same for the exhale.
- Pinch your nose *after* that calm exhalation and start walking, mouth still closed, around the room or the space you're in. Count the number of steps you take. When you are not able to hold your breath any longer, let go of your nose, and inhale through your nose.
- Continue to inhale and exhale calmly through your nose and note how many steps you took. Try to wind down by breathing calmly as soon as possible. If you can't inhale and exhale through your nose, you have pushed yourself too much.

Now for the moment of truth. Anders Olsson is Swedish, so I've translated the breath test results grid.

Health status	Hold breath sitting	Hold breath walking
Optimum health	60 seconds	120+ steps
Very good health	40 seconds	80–100 steps
Good health, issues present when exposed to a trigger	30 seconds	60–80 steps
Poor health, issues often present	20 seconds	40–60 steps
Many different issues present	10 seconds	20–40 steps
Probably on medication/s, disease present, very heavy breathing	3–5 seconds	10–20 steps
Dead	0 seconds	0 steps

How did you do? Unless you're a free diver who's trained to hold their breath for remarkable periods of time, I bet the results were not as encouraging as you'd like them to be . . .

So maybe it's time to learn a bit about breathing and how to do it better. But before we dive into that, let's – literally – take a deep dive, right to the bottom of the sea.

Diving deep

Filming for my series *The Greek Islands with Julia Bradbury* took me to the Dodecanese and the island of Symi, which, rather wonderfully, is named after a nymph who stole the heart of Poseidon, the god of the sea. Looking back over my thirty years on TV, I remember it as one of the most memorable and soul-enhancing jobs I have ever done.

You arrive on a ferry as if you're floating into an opera set where grand houses the colour of sugared almonds line a perfect harbour. They were built with the money that washed over the island when it was home to Greece's sponge-diving fleet. Symi's sponges were used for everything from taking a bath to padding soldiers' helmets and making engineering seals. The only way to harvest them was free-diving, a skill handed down from father to son.

Until, that is, the arrival of the first ever scuba-diving helmet in 1863.

It was a bit of a contraption, one of those great big goldfish bowls with an air hose attached to a boat above, but it was all that was needed to turn Symi into a museum piece rather than a busy trading port. Why? Because it severed the link between how long a human being could hold their breath and how many sponges could be collected and sold. Within a century, they were all gone: the last sponge season on Symi was in the 1960s.

Even though the sponges are almost all gone, you can still find free divers on Symi today. I took to sea with Vasilis and his fifteen-year-old son Ulysses. Vasilis assured me we'd 'only' go eleven or twelve metres down, though that sounded pretty deep to me. Like his forefathers, he can use a 10kg flat stone as a weight and a 'steering wheel' and walk along the seabed, with the stone (called a *skandalopetra*) tucked under his arm like a briefcase. It's incredible to witness.

I watched as he prepared to dive, sitting on the edge of the boat, clearing his mind and, crucially, calming his breath. With our underwater camera, we could see him plunge through the azure blue water. I hoped that, with fifteen years of yoga breathing behind me, I'd manage something similar.

Even though I'd dived and snorkelled many times in my life, I was nervous. I tried to copy Vasilis's dive, but I failed, spearing back up to the surface. It wasn't holding my breath that was the hard part, it was equalising the pressure – I felt as if someone was driving nails into my eardrums. (When you are free-diving, you don't have the luxury of time to get used to the pressure, as you do in scuba gear.) But I had spotted a beautiful dark sponge on the sea bed, and the idea of being able to gently touch this primitive sea creature encouraged me to try again.

On my second attempt, I made it.

For a few seconds, I was able to look up through the water shimmering above me, though it wasn't long before I needed to scissor-kick my way back to the surface to draw a breath. I was elated in a way I couldn't quite put my finger on.

'You have returned to your mother – the sea is our mother, the feeling is strong,' said Vasilis.

He and Ulysses made a big impression on me. I was deeply envious of their freedom and the love and respect they had for the elements. They were two of the calmest and most empathetic humans I have ever met. Obviously, their island lifestyle helps, but if this is what breathwork does for you, then it's blissful.

It was that trip to Symi and my encounter with them that made me start to take breath more seriously. I'd used it to work my way into yoga poses and hold them, but I began to understand how breathwork could also improve my physical and mental health. I know that free-diving for sponges has gone forever from Symi – Vasilis wasn't wrong when he described it as 'an environmental disaster' – but I do think the islanders' super-power still has a place in today's world.

Check out the work of the appropriately named Ocean Ramsey, a Hawaii-based marine conservationist, scuba instructor and model. She's an expert free diver famous for swimming with sharks, including a twenty-foot Great White, one of the biggest ever recorded. There's footage of it on YouTube. You can see her clasp the shark's left fin and go for a graceful tow, absolutely at one with an apex predator, and remarkably there's no equipment in sight, she is *free diving*.

I'm not suggesting you join Ocean in swimming with sharks, but breathwork can work its magic in all our lives. I have come to depend on it since my cancer diagnosis – it's now an integral part of my morning routine.

The nose knows

It sits in the middle of your face. Moistens and warms incoming air. Breathes it back out when you've used it. That's probably as much as most of us know.

So here are some less familiar facts.

The average male has a nose size of 2.2 inches; the average female nose size is 2 inches, but this protrusion has hidden depths. The nasal cavity behind the real estate on display is about 6 cubic inches, the size of a small fist.

The interior is coated with erectile tissue, the same type of flesh that covers the penis, clitoris and nipples. And all those hairs you fret about are filters for germs and bacteria. Trillions of molecules of air pass through our noses with every sniff, so do learn to love them.

Your beating heart

If you catch me on television these days, you'll see I wear a Garmin smartwatch. It's one of the bits of equipment I have invested in to increase my understanding of my body post-cancer.

I have never regarded myself as an anxious person, but as I said in Chapter 1, I have learned that stress comes packaged in many forms and we are all impacted by it. I hadn't acknowledged the stress I was under in my work (much as I love it), what with the deadlines, the public scrutiny, the emails, the logistics, the lack of sleep and hopping between time zones.

I wanted to get a wearable so I could keep track of myself. Since strapping it on to my wrist, I've found the most useful functions are the stress and heart-rate variability (HRV) monitors (and of course the step counter! My goal is 10,000 most days).

HRV is a measure of the variation in time between each heartbeat. This variation is controlled by the autonomic nervous system, which, as the name suggests, works 'automatically' behind the scenes regulating functions like our heart rate, blood pressure, breathing and digestion.

It can indicate any number of issues, ranging from a heart condition to anxiety, depression and stress. I now know if I've been pushing myself too hard when I'm filming and travelling, because my HRV drops a few points. The same thing happens if I have a few bad nights' sleep in a row.

When we're in a fight-or-flight mode the variation between the subsequent heartbeats tends to be lower. When the autonomic nervous system is in a more relaxed state, the variation between beats may be higher, and you get a higher HRV reading.

The accuracy of these devices is still under scrutiny but generally chest strap monitors are regarded as being a more accurate measure of HRV than wrist devices. Regardless, it's an interesting and non-invasive way to track how your nervous system is reacting, not just to the bodily environment but also to emotions, thoughts and feelings.

It shows you how easy it is to upset the equilibrium of our bodies. But if we know about it, we can set ourselves back on course and rebalance, using breath.

Our autonomic nervous system is working 24/7. Think of it as a super-computer that runs a lot of the processes in the body. It regulates your heartbeat and digestion, but also controls your emotions, your behaviour, your sex drive and your breathing. Breathing is what I want to focus on here, because it is the *only* process within that system that we can consciously control.

We can choose to stop breathing (up to a point) or to breathe faster. We can choose to implement specific breathing patterns. So even though you can't directly tell your nervous system 'Release more serotonin!' to help you feel good, you *can* achieve the same outcome by introducing a breathing practice to calm it down. (Interestingly, around seventy-five per cent of people struggling with anxiety have disordered breathing.)

What's been a surprise for me is how situations that I'd expect to be putting my body under stress are a breeze. I'm breathing well and handling the pace. At other times, the Garmin shows my stress levels to be surprisingly high, and the way to deal with that is through breathwork.

The golden rule is that my exhalation must be longer than my inhalation, to calm me down. A longer exhalation sends a message to the brain to activate the parasympathetic nervous system, the 'rest and digest' mode, which is the opposite of the sympathetic nervous system (which is anything but sympathetic!), the 'fight, flight or freeze' mode.

So, I breathe in (through my nose) for four and out for six, and it sets my body back to rights. I inhale as if I'm smelling a flower and exhale out through the nose quite noisily, in a circular pattern – no pause between breaths, mouth closed. I do this for about five minutes, sometimes ten, but if you find it uncomfortable I suggest starting off for one minute daily for a week, slowly increasing the duration through the month. It's called resonance or coherence breathing and it slows down the breath rate, which has an impact that lasts beyond the actual practice time. I've seen my HRV increase (which is a good thing remember) by up to three points the morning after a session. Slowing your breathing to about five cycles per minute is a breathing cycle that many people use for meditation – as I've already said, most of us breathe too fast at around twelve to eighteen times a minute. You can experiment with different ratios too: inhale four exhale four, inhale five exhale five, inhale five exhale seven, inhale six exhale six. As with meditation, it's important to experiment and find what works for you. Your intention is what transforms the practice – attention energises, intention transforms.

I recently completed a day's filming in Ireland with Professor Shane O'Mara, the neuroscientist and passionate walker who heads the Trinity College Institute of Neuroscience in Dublin.

We were walking home together through the Dublin suburb of Sandycove, which, as its name suggests, is along the coast. I have a really clear memory of the moment, right down to what I was wearing: a roll-neck sweater and a big yellow puffer jacket. The sun was shining, the surroundings were beautiful, and the interview was fascinating. We'd even had time to stop for lunch – it was a far less punishing schedule than some of my other shoots. It could hardly have been more perfect.

Yet, when I glanced at my Garmin, my stress levels had rocketed, showing that even doing the best job in the world on the loveliest day was still putting my mind and body under pressure. I had invested a hundred per cent in that filming, and alongside all my passion and positivity, there came stress. I am not saying this job is as stressful as making your living through hard manual labour or saving lives in an operating theatre, I am simply making the point that we can all underestimate how our bodies constantly respond to everyday pressures.

I went for dinner to a local Indian restaurant recommended by Shane. It was jam-packed. We grabbed the last table, and I took two minutes to do some quiet breathwork, without disturbing other diners. I closed my eyes, put my hands gently on my lap, and started breathing through my nose, counting in for four beats, holding for four beats and then breathing out for eight beats.

By the time the veg curry arrived, my Garmin was telling me that order had been restored.

James's story: The healing pond

At the top of author James Erith's Essex garden was an old farmyard where nothing grew from beneath the layers of concrete, tarmac and flint. In 2015, he decided to dig it up and build a swimming pond as a haven for wildlife – and hopefully for his family, too.

Just as a mechanical digger was making its first cut, James, then forty-five, snapped his Achilles tendon in a game of village cricket. It was 'like a rifle shot going off', he recalls, and he recognised the potentially devastating consequences of his injury. He'd already had three previous surgeries on his knee.

'In hospital, just as I was being led into theatre, a young doctor pleaded with me not to proceed with the operation. He could see I was in poor physical shape. I was verging on obese, something I hadn't dared to confront. I agreed and pulled out. It was an extraordinary moment.'

Back home, however, he was in trouble.

'I struggled to walk. My foot was in a cast that kept my toes en pointe like a ballet dancer. I developed a terrible gut reaction to my medications. At night, I ground my teeth to the nerves and my head was filled with electric tooth pain. Every part of me hurt. I was falling apart and there was nothing I could do except take more pills.

'I was terrified of turning into one of those people who slip down the pharmaceutical funnel, filling up their pill organisers every week, until they can't return.'

As James searched for what he calls 'an alternative way of pulling myself together', the dig was finished and the skeleton of the pond was built. It felt like a small victory.

Two days later, a violent summer storm struck and devastated the site.

'I felt a strange synergy with my pond,' says James. 'It looked as if it had been blown up. I knew I couldn't go on. I was searching for some magical solution, but deep down I accepted such a thing didn't exist. Whatever was going to fix this had to come from me.'

Online, he discovered the work of extreme athlete and breathing expert Wim Hof, whose healing techniques rely on breathwork, exposure to cold and meditation. With the pond build under way again, James realised that having a swimming pond at the end of his garden would enable him to practise all three.

He began with breathwork, and was astonished at the instant results. 'Those breathing rounds – I was blown away by how powerful they were.'

Next, he tackled his weight issue. 'I looked at my food intake and decided the time had come to give up sugar. I started making kefir and read frantically about diets. Nothing resonated until I read about intermittent fasting. For me, it was a super-powerful technique. In a month, I lost a stone and found my mind was so much clearer.

'It was as if I'd sparked a fragment of life energy I'd somehow neglected. But my Achilles – that still wasn't fixed. The pain tore at the tendon as if it was being put through a mangle.'

James turned to meditation to try to take control of his pain without drugs. He also began a daily regime of rigorous stretching following a simple but effective programme known as the Five Tibetan Rites. Slowly, with time and gentle exercise, he was able to rehabilitate his leg and foot.

Over the winter, the pond started filling up and, on a lovely spring evening, James prepared to take his first swim.

'First I blessed my new pond. It felt perfect. The water was around ten degrees, but controlling my breath, I did several lengths and emerged euphoric, absolutely buzzing. Perhaps the cold is about beating a tiny bit of fear. It makes you feel completely alive.'

By summer, James was back playing cricket and spent the

light nights wading around other people's ponds, thinning out their plants and making his car stink with sludge as he dragged them home to populate his own pond.

The first swallows had appeared in early May; by June and July, dragonflies were buzzing up and down and bees were humming in the spoil bank, which was filled with nepeta (catnip). As James swam, water-bugs shuttled around him and newts plunged to the depths to escape.

'Even the heron popped in every now and then to check if any fish had arrived,' he remembers. 'Nature flourished.'

And so did James. Building and using his healing pond (the title of the book he's written about the experience), James lost three stones, and learned how to breathe, stretch and take a cold shower or have a chilly swim every day. Now he is rarely sick and hasn't taken a painkiller for four years.

'Through the natural beauty hidden beneath that old concrete, I found myself,' he says. 'I found my spirit – my other self, my health, my appreciation for the outdoors and the pure joy of being human.'

Breathing is the first thing we do when we are born and the last thing we do as we die. Like proper sleep and good nutrition, it's one of the pillars of your life. You just have to know how to get the best out of it. The world's breathing experts might disagree about how to do that – there are many different methods – but they are united in the belief that we all need to try. That's where Patrick McKeown and Oxygen Advantage come in. Patrick is the creator and CEO of Oxygen Advantage, one of the best-known breath-training programmes in the world. Patrick himself walks a lot – he moved to a remote location in rural west Ireland so he could breathe more easily, in all senses. At the end of the chapter, on page 148, you'll find an exclusive breathing exercise he's created for you to enjoy while walking.

Patrick struggled so much at school that he dropped out at

fourteen years of age before eventually returning, going on to university and then into the corporate world. He was plagued by asthma and breathing issues, to the point where people often thought he had a bad cold. He was on permanent medication and had been hospitalised, too. His sleep was poor, his stress levels sky-high.

It was back in 1998 that he discovered a nose unblocking exercise, which simply involves holding the breath. This exercise is described at the end of this chapter so you can try it for yourself. Practising this exercise, along with breathing through the nose during rest and exercise, helped free up his nose to the point that he could use it comfortably. To ensure he was nose breathing during sleep, he wore a nasal dilator, a little plastic strip to help open his nose, and taped his mouth closed. (Waking up with a moist mouth in the morning is confirmation that the mouth is closed during sleep.) This helped him have a refreshing, deeper sleep and wake up in better form and more alert to start the day. Since this was before the age of the internet, Patrick simply stumbled across it in a newspaper article, but the impact was extraordinary. Within two days, he was having the best sleep of his life, and within two weeks, his wheezing was down fifty per cent. Today, his life is dedicated to teaching everyone from pro athletes to asthmatic children how to breathe better.

I sat down with Patrick to learn more about breathing.

A conversation with Patrick McKeown

We're not breathing properly, are we?

Patrick: Not all of us! Lots of people breathe orally instead of nasally, or a little faster and harder into the upper chest. The nose is the only organ in the human body that does anything in terms of the breath; the mouth has no purpose other than to allow air straight down the throat and into our lungs. Open your mouth, look into it and ask yourself what part of it is dedicated to breathing? None! It's your nose that does all the real work. It increases oxygen uptake in the blood, and improves oxygen delivery to your tissues and organs. It can influence your blood circulation. The air is drawn into the lower regions of the lungs due to improved recruitment of the diaphragm. This is the main breathing muscle, and plays a number of roles including calming the mind, massaging the internal organs and providing stabilisation to the spine. This all starts with the nose, so it's critically important to get back to nasal breathing, both when you are awake and asleep. It's not a magic bullet, but we can improve the function of vital organs and body systems, and our mental health, by changing our breathing patterns.

How can I gauge my current breathing?

Patrick: Can you breathe comfortably through your nose while jogging or doing other moderate physical exercise? Then you're pretty good! If you feel air hunger even when you're resting, then you have work to do. Breathing should be effortless. Start by breathing in and out through your nose. Pay attention to your breathing and be conscious of not breathing too much air. This is the first step to improving breathing patterns. The second step is to learn to breathe light and slow, and then deep. An easy way to remember this might be light, slow and deep (LSD). But remember, breathing deep just means drawing air into the lower regions of the lungs. When it comes to breathing – deep and big are not the same thing.

What, no puffing and panting like you see on the internet?

Patrick: I often wonder why the idea of taking the full deep breath is so prevalent in our society. What purpose does it serve? No animal is purposely filling their lungs with air in the erroneous belief that it will bring more oxygen throughout the body. Have you ever seen your dog or cat intentionally breathing harder and faster? They breathe as nature intended, and for the most part that is in and out through the nose with a breathing volume that serves their body requirements at that time. Taking the full breath might bring temporary relief by eliminating a feeling of discomfort or air hunger. But, long term, it could be the worst thing to be doing because it will expel too much carbon dioxide from the lungs. Carbon dioxide is our primary driver to breathe, not oxygen. It comes from the tissues into the blood and accumulates in our lungs, but some of us are overly sensitive to it. Those of us with a history of trauma or high stress, panic disorder or anxiety feel that we are not getting enough air. This sensation of air hunger can be due to increased sensitivity to carbon dioxide. Decreasing this sensitivity makes us breathe better.

Trendy techniques that involve taking big, loud, deep breaths – in other words, hyperventilation – can be helpful for some people. When practised correctly, breathing this way for short periods of time stresses the body to cause positive adaptations.

More importantly, however, is how we breathe every day – during rest, sleep and physical exercise. If one is habitually breathing a little faster, harder and into the upper chest during rest and sleep – this can impair oxygen delivery and trigger a constant fight-or-flight response. I know when we go into the gym, we see people huffing and puffing away with their mouths open, even during low-intensity exercise. But our mouths are not for breathing, our mouths are for eating, drinking and talking.

You mentioned carbon dioxide . . .

Patrick: If we breathe in too much air and get rid of too much carbon dioxide, then our haemoglobin, which is the main carrier of oxygen in the blood, clings on to its oxygen and doesn't release it to the tissues and organs. This discovery was made over one hundred years ago and is called the Bohr effect. So not only is our blood circulation impaired but our oxygen delivery is, too. It also increases our blood pH, giving us something called respiratory alkalosis. (It's the air we breathe, not the food we eat, which makes our blood acid or alkaline, no matter what faddy diet you read about.) Respiratory alkalosis arouses the central nervous system which includes the brain then puts us into fight-or-flight mode – and that's not good.

Finally, the old saying 'cold hands, warm heart', is rubbish. As carbon dioxide leaves the blood, the blood vessels constrict, so it's very common for people to have cold hands and cold feet. Cold hands are not the sign of a warm heart – they're a sign of dysfunctional breathing!

What are we aiming for, then?

Patrick: You need to have all three dimensions of breathing in harmony. There's the biochemical dimension, which is carbon dioxide in the blood and our sensitivity to this gas; the biomechanical dimension, which is whether someone is breathing high with the upper chest, or low, with good recruitment of the diaphragm; and finally, there's the psycho-physiological dimension, which is the two-way connection between the body and the mind.

And how do we get there?

Patrick: I'm always extolling the virtues of getting out for a walk in green spaces. Going for a walk is an opportune time to train the physical body, the mind, and our breathing. At the start of your walk, remind yourself that this is your time – to take attention out of the head and into the body, or onto your breathing. Give yourself some attention – your body is craving it. And then start breathing all through the nose. It is as simple as that. Even if you feel uncomfortable placing your attention on your breathing, don't worry. Do your gardening, yoga or any movement with your mouth closed and forget about your breathing. Increasing oxygen uptake in the blood and bringing your body and mind into a state of calmness is all you need to do to make a start.

How do we breathe if we are walking briskly or running in those green spaces?

Patrick: I would still encourage you to breathe in and out through your nose. Allow your nose to determine the pace. Doing exercise while breathing nasally gets easier, because the body adapts to the increased carbon dioxide and your air hunger diminishes. Remember that carbon dioxide is the primary driver of breathing. It can take a few weeks. If there's a point where the intensity of the exercise gets too much, then yes, you could switch to breathing in through the nose and out of the mouth, but you should still come back to nose breathing when you can. You're causing your body to make positive adaptations, to improve your breathing patterns. Once you have set them, they will remain for the rest of the day and while you are asleep.

How should I breathe to ensure a calming start to my morning?

Patrick: Begin by moving your body, walking or yoga or any movement for that matter. Breathe in and out through your nose. After a few minutes of movement, exhale through your nose and pinch your nose with your fingers to hold your breath. Continue moving while holding your breath for five to ten paces (or about five seconds to generate a feeling of slight breathlessness). Then resume breathing in and out through your nose. Continue moving with nasal breathing for half a minute and repeat the breath hold. Repeat ten times throughout your movement. Holding the breath on the exhalation for a few seconds during physical movement will help open your nose and improve blood flow to the brain. This is a great wake up, as well as making breathing easier.

How should I breathe before I have a tricky meeting with my boss?

Patrick: When we are facing a challenge, the main thing is not to hyperventilate. When we hyperventilate, we are breathing faster or harder, and into the upper chest. That's the body telling the brain things are not OK. So, if you're going in to talk to the boss, don't let yourself hyperventilate beforehand, because all your brain will want to do is to get your body away from the threat. Instead, bring your attention to your breathing and think about the speed of your exhalation, which should be about one and a half to two times the length of your inhalation. Take a normal silent breath in through your nose and allow a very soft and slow gentle breath out through your nose. There is no need to time your breathing. It's the speed of that out-breath which determines whether you're telling the brain that you're feeling calm or stressed. By allowing a gentle and slow breath out, the body is telling the brain that everything is OK, and the brain in turns sends signals of calm to the body. So let's give this one a go. Nobody will see or hear anything. Practise first in small situations so that you can revert to it during more challenging situations. Don't worry about doing it perfectly, and even if you feel that nothing is happening, take comfort in the knowledge that it is working for you in the background. Personally, whenever I am met with a challenging situation, this is my go-to exercise. It only takes thirty seconds to elicit a relaxation response, but try to keep going for ninety seconds – that's even better.

What if it's a really tricky meeting?

Patrick: If people are comfortable with it, and if they feel OK, they could try breathing in for four seconds and out for six. So, breathe in silently through the nose for one, two, three, four and out for one, two, three, four, five, six. Slowing down the breath to about six breaths per minute elicits a relaxation response and brings the body and mind into balance. If your breathing is a little challenging, then slowing down the rate to six breaths per minute might be too difficult. Instead, you could breathe in for two seconds and out for three seconds (twelve breaths per minute) or in for three seconds and out for five seconds (seven and half breaths per minute). The main thing is that you are breathing in and out through your nose, with a soft silent inhale and a slow, relaxed and gentle exhale. That's all.

What if it's a really, really tricky meeting?

Patrick: When stress is off the scale, this exercise will help get you back in control of your mind and your emotions. It activates the vagus nerve, boosts blood flow and oxygen delivery to the brain, takes your attention away from overthinking and calms the brain. Take a normal breath, in through your nose and out through your nose. Now pinch your nose and hold it for a count of five, four, three, two, one, then let go and breathe in again through your nose. Now just breathe normally for two to three breaths. These are simple, small breath holds. And again, take a normal breath in through your nose, out through your nose, then pinch your nose and hold, for five, four, three, two, one, and then let go. Then breathe in through your nose and now just breathe normally for two to three breaths – that's around ten to fifteen seconds, depending on the speed of breathing. It's very simple and very effective. Everybody can do it, there are no side effects. Practise for about five to ten minutes, at the start of the day. You can use it every hour if you need to.

I'm going live on TV in an hour. I need to be calm but energised. What should I do?

Patrick: If you're feeling tired, close your eyes and direct them upwards, as if there's a roof light at the top of your head. This shifts the attention in the brain away from the frontal area, which is the seat of critical thinking, towards the centre or the back of the head. Then bring your attention to your breathing, taking a soft silent breath in and exhaling with a simple, slow, relaxed breath. Do that for five to ten minutes (or as long as necessary), in order to feel re-energised. The next step is to target the biomechanical dimension of breathing we talked about earlier. Place your hands on either side of your lower ribs. As you breathe in and out, feel the lower ribs gently moving.

The objective is to achieve a state where you have just the right amount of nerves – you are alert and relaxed at the same time, with the critical mind set aside and your focus solely on the task at hand. Too many nerves will scare the life out of us, and people have experienced panic attacks on live TV, or on stage – the result of hyperventilation.

The next step is to breathe in softly for four seconds, hold the breath for four seconds, breathe out softly for four seconds and hold the breath for four seconds. This is called box breathing or tactical breathing as it is used by special forces and police prior to an operation. If a soldier or a police officer is too stressed, they are more likely to make a mistake and it could cost a life. Hence the importance for everyone to be able to self-regulate.

Or you could breathe in and out through your nose, pinch it closed, and then keep holding it while you walk around your dressing room, holding your breath as you go. That's a stressor; it opens up the nose, increases blood flow to the brain, and wakens you out of relaxation mode. Do it until you feel a moderate to strong air hunger. (If you are pregnant, don't try this. If you suffer from anxiety or a panic disorder, go gently, because it is a stressor exercise.) Then walk out there and enjoy yourself.

[Obviously, that last exercise applies to any situation where you need to be turbo-charged but not frazzled. Mine is doing live TV where there are no second takes. You will know what yours is, for sure. I imagine you are thinking about it right now.]

Mouth-breathing

The science journalist James Nestor learned all about the downside of breathing through your mouth when he went in search of answers to his regular bouts of pneumonia and bronchitis. You can discover what he found out in his brilliant book *Breath*. (The abridged version: mouth-breathing is really bad for you.)

He was part of an experiment at Stanford University looking at how much damage might be caused if a person were to breathe exclusively through their mouth for ten days. After the snot was removed, Nestor's nose was sealed tight with silicone plugs and surgical tape. By the end of this horrible-sounding experiment, his blood pressure had risen by an average of thirteen points, he had twenty-five apnoea events (which amount to mini-choking episodes) while sleeping, and some pretty unpleasant bacteria had infected the skin on his face.

The book's biggest takeaway is that you should breathe through your nose. And yet, Nestor writes, 'around half of us are habitual mouth-breathers', due to the way the human skull has evolved over the last 300,000 years, and especially in the last 500 years.

This, says Nestor, was the biggest surprise in his research: that our jaws and teeth have gone into a kind of semi-retirement since processed food became our staple diet. Essentially, with the onset of the industrial age, our faces caved in. Our mouths shrank, our nasal passages became more constricted, and our airways suffered the shortfall.

'Even if we want to breathe properly, so many of us are so messed up anatomically now that it's a real struggle,' he says.

The universal language of breath

So now we know breathing through the nose is important – but we're definitely not on to anything new.

An American artist called George Catlin explored the Great Plains of the US back in the 1830s. He lived with, painted and studied fifty Native American tribes. Even though they differed from region to region, they shared one striking characteristic: their teeth were as 'regular as the keys of a piano', according to Catlin.

These tribes all believed that breathing through the mouth sapped the body of strength and was responsible for stress and disease. Children were taught to nose-breathe from birth, with parents and guardians pinching babies' lips closed if their mouths opened while they slept. Some adults wouldn't even smile with an open mouth, for fear air might find its way in. (This story is beautifully told by James Nestor in *Breath*.)

You can find references to our precious nostrils in medical texts dating back to 1500 BCE and in the folds of ancient Chinese Taoist papers. And you'll also find that the language used around them down the millennia is a clue to their importance.

Around the world, the word for breath is often the same as the word for life, spirit and soul. The Latin word *spiritum*, meaning 'breath' gives us the word 'spirit' in English. In Greek, the word *pneuma* translates to 'air' or 'breath' and can also mean 'spirit' or 'life energy'. *Prana* is the Sanskrit word for 'air' and 'breath' and also means 'sacred essence of life'. *Ha* is what the Hawaiian people call breath, and this is connected to the word *mana*, which means 'spiritual force'. In Asia, we see the same pattern. The word *chi* is used in Chinese medicine to mean 'breath' and 'air', while also meaning the 'universal and cosmic energy of life'. In Japan, *ki* is a similar concept, and is invoked in the martial arts.

Different cultures practise a variety of breathing techniques for spiritual ceremonies or on journeys of self-discovery. Women in the Kalahari, for example, use communal dancing and breath-work to reach a state of ecstasy. After several hours of high-energy dancing, they shorten their breath to create an oxygen deficiency, and pass out (sounds like so many parties I've been to!).

Here are some more kinds of breathing from around the world. You will have to investigate them further yourself if you'd like to try any, but I hope that by showing you the span of countries and cultures that revere breath, you'll be curious to know more.

Medical note: You must consult a doctor if you are pregnant or have any medical issues such as high blood pressure, heart or lung problems, or anything wrong with your eyes and ears.

Do not try any of these breathing practices without taking appropriate medical advice.

Tibet: *Tummo*

Tummo means 'inner fire' and is an ancient meditation technique practised by monks in Tibetan Buddhism. It's a combination of breathing and visualisation, and can be used to increase inner heat. (Some people say today's Wim Hof Method is *tummo* but he sees his technique as unique and different. Nevertheless Wim has raised awareness globally and I doubt we'd all be writing about breath so prolifically without his influence. His ability to control bodily functions via breathwork has been described as extraordinary.) *Tummo* was pioneered by an Indian man named Naropa in the tenth century. He is said to have stopped himself freezing to death while living in a cave in Kathmandu, Nepal, using the power of his breath. It might sound implausible, but a famous experiment in the 1980s, overseen by an associate professor of medicine at Harvard Medical School, saw Tibetan monks placed in a cold room (at a brrrr-inducing 4°C), and enter a deep state of meditation using the *tummo* technique. They were covered in wet sheets, which would usually cause hypothermia – even death, in some people – but soon the sheets started to steam because of their body heat. The 'laundry' was dry in about an hour.[2]

India, the home of breathwork:
Pranayama

Pranayama, the Indian technique of breath control, comes from Sanskrit, where *prana* means 'life energy' and *yama* means 'control'. Invented by Shiva about 7,000 years ago, it's a big part of yoga. Early morning and late evening are the most beneficial times for practice. Common sense suggests you choose energising exercises to set you up for the day, and slow, calming exercises to wind you down in the evening. I'll let you delve into what works best for you, but here are some basics to get you going.

Diaphragmatic breath or belly breathing: This is the beginner's exercise. Place one hand on your upper chest and the other just below your ribcage. Breathe in slowly through your nose so your stomach moves out against your hand. Tighten your stomach muscles so that your stomach moves back in and exhale through pursed lips. This encourages full oxygen exchange – oxygen in and carbon dioxide out – which will slow your heartbeat and can help stabilise your blood pressure.

Dirga pranayama (three-part or complete breath): This strengthens and expands on diaphragmatic breathing. The three-part breath improves breath awareness and lung capacity. Inhale from the low belly (just under your belly button), then the low chest (the lower half of the ribcage) and then the low throat (just above the top of your sternum). Exhale starting at the top, and work your way back down. It's done continuously and through your nose.

Sama vritti pranayama (equal breath): This basic breath focuses on an inhalation, a breath hold, and an exhalation, all for the same length. It is balancing and deeply relaxing – and very good for beginners. Inhale and exhale through your nose in a slow, even and continuous flow, using your diaphragmatic breathing. Then inhale for a count of four, hold your breath for a count of four, exhale for a count of four and hold your breath again for a count of four. Repeat the cycle for another two to six rounds of breath (this should sound familiar, because it's the box breathing that Patrick mentioned).

Nadi shodhana pranayama (alternate nostril breathing): This intermediate practice involves breathing through one nostril at a time to bring harmony and balance. Place your forefinger and your middle finger in the middle of your eyebrows, at the 'third eye'. Close your right nostril with your thumb (your ring finger and pinky finger should be free, hovering). Exhale through the left nostril, then inhale through the same left nostril. Hold the breath for a beat. Then place your ring finger and pinky finger over your left nostril, closing it, and release the thumb from the right nostril, while exhaling from the right nostril. Then inhale through the same right nostril. Then place the thumb back on the right nostril to close it. Exhale out of the left nostril, releasing the ring finger and pinky finger. Inhale again through the same left nostril, closing the right nostril again with the thumb. That's one round. It is a lot simpler than it sounds, though you'll need to practise at first. I incorporate this into my breathwork practice most mornings.

Not all breathing techniques are ancient. *Sudarshan Kriya* is the new kid on the block, born in the 1980s, at around the same time Joe Cocker was taking us 'Up Where We Belong' and Roxy Music were telling us we were 'More Than This'. Most examples of *pranayama*, are, however, several millennia old, but remain very effective in today's world. Here are some that are ubiquitous in yoga classes globally. (I'm a fan.)

1. *Ujjayi* or 'victorious breath'. Breathe in through your nose so your breath catches on the back of your throat, and breathe out, also through your nose. The length of your exhale should match the length of your inhale. Try to breathe from your diaphragm. This should be a smooth motion with no pause or breath retention between breaths. This gives you excellent control of your breath cycle, and will make you mentally and physically calm, but extra alert. (Sometimes this is referred to as 'Darth Vader' breath.)

2. *Bhastrika* or 'bellows breath'. Inhale and exhale forcefully at a rate of thirty breaths per minute. It requires powerful and rapid inhalations and exhalations through the nose which you can clearly hear. It is called the bellows breath because the abdomen pumps in and out like the bellows of a blacksmith. Your arms are also used to help with the 'bellows' motion: lift your arms so your elbows are in line with your shoulders, and your hands, gently clenched into fists, are in line with your ears. Your forearms should be facing forwards. As you inhale through your nose, into your belly, raise your fists in the air, so your arms are straight above you, and open your palms. Exhale energetically out of your nostrils and bring your arms quickly back down to your sides, clenching your hands back into fists.

This action mimics a 'pumping' motion to 'force' the air out of your body. A full inhalation and exhalation count as one round and can be practised multiple times depending on the aim of your practice. This kind of breathing is good for clearing the airways and increasing energy levels in the body and mind. You will be stimulated and then feel a deep calm.

3. **Chanting.** Chant 'Om' three times over a long, extended exhale. It is used in breathwork and yoga practices around the world. It is a way of tuning in to our higher selves, connecting to the universe and deepening whichever practice you are enjoying, breathwork or meditation. It is a sacred sound, pronounced Ah-uu-mm, and chanting it has a positive and calming effect on the brain and central nervous system. This all might sound a bit woo-woo to you, but humming – and you could argue that chanting 'om' is a form of humming – increases nitric oxide (NO). We know from this chapter that nitric oxide has a range of health benefits. It is known to be broadly anti-fungal, anti-viral and anti-bacterial. So, it can help protect the body by sterilising airborne pathogens. It also plays an important role in the dilation of blood vessels so that oxygen can be properly distributed through the body. Interestingly, it has been suggested that there is a specific frequency that creates more nitric oxide, which is 120 hertz, which is actually, on the musical scale, the key of B! So, identify your favourite Taylor Swift track and hum it to the key of B for a few minutes every day, if you don't fancy chanting 'om'.

Do I sound like I'm joking? I'm not! In 1998, Louis Ignarro, Robert F Furchgott and Ferid Murad won the Nobel Prize in medicine for their research showing how nitric oxide supports cardiovascular health. Since these discoveries, many more links to nitric oxide have been made, including how it assists in brain function, decreases muscle soreness and increases exercise performance. So get humming or OMMMMMing, whichever floats your boat (always consult your doctor first, though). I've added this to my morning routine and hum my way around the house, much to the amusement of my family.

China: *Dantian* breathing

Dantian, or *dan tian*, translates to 'field of elixir' and is rooted in Taoist and Buddhist traditions. In traditional Chinese medicine, *dantian* are considered to be energy centres that hold the 'three treasures of the body', *jing*, *qi* and *shen*. These are described as the energies that support and sustain the blood, bodily fluids and solid tissues.[3]

There are three main *dantian* in the body:

- the lower *dantian* – this is approximately two fingers' width below your belly button
- the middle *dantian* – this is around your solar plexus
- the upper *dantian* – this is in your forehead, between your eyebrows

The basics of dantian *breathing*

1. Stand with your back straight and your feet planted on the ground, shoulder-width apart. Your knees should be slightly bent, not locked, and your pelvic floor pulled forward.
2. Imagine a string running from the crown of your head through your body and down to the ground between your feet. Place your hands over the lower *dantian*.
3. With every inhale, draw the breath deeply into the lower *dantian*, feeling it expand with air and energy.
4. Continue for five minutes, letting your mind rest on that area while you are breathing The lower *dantian* is the focus because it is thought to house our energy and power. It nourishes the other two *dantians*.

Greece: *Pneuma* breathwork

The ancient Greeks believed in the power of an energy called *pneuma*, not dissimilar to Chinese *chi*. They had lots of different theories about it – some contradictory – but the general idea was that *pneuma* was necessary for the functioning of vital organs and also acted as the bridge between body and soul. Legend has it that a boxer accomplished in the practice of *pneuma* breathwork could use his outstretched fingers to hit his opponent's abdomen hard enough to burst their stomach wall. Then he'd tear out their guts. Nice.[4]

As mentioned earlier in the chapter, Patrick McKeown has created a breathing exercise with real impact that could be incorporated into any daily walk and then built on to increase the benefits.

Breathing clever

Walk at a pace where you can sustain nasal breathing. In the first few weeks, the sensation of air hunger might be a little strong and your nose may run. These are minor and temporary inconveniences. Before you know it, breathing in and out through your nose during exercise will be the most natural thing in the world for you.

Walking is a time to take attention out of the head and on to the breath. It is not a time to be spent lost in thought, ruminating and dwelling on what has happened or what might happen. As you walk, bring your full focus to your breathing. Feel the slightly colder air entering your nostrils and the slightly warmer air leaving your nose.

Focused attention on the breath is the perfect way to help anchor the mind. Any time the mind wanders off, bring your attention back to your breathing. This is training for the brain and improves your ability to hold attention – first on the breath and then in everyday life.

Bring your attention to your body. With lips together and jaws relaxed, breathe in and out through your nose in a regular and easy manner. Allow your breathing to soften relative to what you feel you need. A tolerable sensation of air hunger is the goal. If the sensation of breathlessness or air hunger is too much, simply slow down to a pace that is right for you.

Remind yourself to breathe softly and slowly on every breath. Know that breathing too much air causes blood vessels to constrict, activates the body's stress response, and reduces oxygen delivery to the heart, brain and rest of the body. To help ensure optimal oxygen delivery to your muscles and organs, reduce the volume of air you take in. Only breathe what you need.

When you are comfortable with light and slow breathing through the nose, bring your attention to your lower ribs. This is the location of the diaphragm breathing muscle. You'll find it towards the bottom of the ribs, where the chest is separated from the abdomen. It can be helpful to place your hands on either side of your body at the lower ribs to get a feel for where the diaphragm is located.

Continue with light, slow nasal breathing while walking. As you breathe in, guide your lower ribs to gently move outwards, and as you breathe out, guide your lower ribs to gently move inwards. Breathing with a good recruitment of the diaphragm helps to bring calmness to the mind and provides stabilisation of the spine.

Breathing through the nose during physical exercise brings your walk to another level, improving your breathing patterns and your sleep, and eliciting a calmer state of mind.

6

Walking and Healing

'Life is lumpy. And a lump in the oatmeal, a lump in
the throat, and a lump in the breast are not the same lump.
One should learn the difference . . .'
Robert Fulghum, *Uh-oh: Some Observations
from Both Sides of the Refrigerator Door*

The London plane tree that stands outside my bathroom window
has been my friend and confidante for the past two years. I have long
admired its camouflage bark, and now I understand its trickery, I
love it even more. Trees make great listeners, and when I do my gratitude practice a few times a week, I always say thank you to my tree.

Despite its name, the species is not native to Britain; it's the
offspring of the American and Oriental planes. Nonetheless, it's a
robust specimen that has adapted brilliantly to survive in crowded
cities such as London, its roots sprawling beneath concrete and
tarmac in an unlikely, unseen and under-appreciated tumble of
twists and turns deep in the ground.

Trees are essential to town planning; they're welcome 'green
breaks' for all of us who live and work in an urban environment.
They suck up pollution and give out oxygen, provide shade and
create wildlife habitats. They even cool our cities' streets by less-
ening what is known as the 'heat island effect' where the built
environment absorbs and retains heat, increasing air pollution
and causing heat-related illnesses.

The London plane hasn't only evolved so its roots survive in the concrete, it also sheds its skin to rid itself of the grubby old smog that accumulates in its bark.

You could say it heals itself. And trees, it turns out, are pretty good at this.

A hollow yew, for example, can regenerate by producing new roots from its centre. Those roots are its scouts, burrowing down in search of new earth to feed and strengthen the ageing tree, prolonging its survival long after many other species would have perished.

Understandably, given this amazing ability, the yew is revered as a symbol of life, rebirth and regeneration.

Unlike trees, we humans don't really know how to fix ourselves as we go. After we're broken, then it suddenly becomes a priority.

I certainly took my own health for granted. My GP, who's cared for me since I was eighteen, has been known to call me 'medically boring' on occasion in the past because so little ailed me on a day-to-day basis. Or so I thought.

It wasn't until Dr Nasha Winters, author of *The Metabolic Approach to Cancer*, written with Jess Higgins Kelley, encouraged me to interrogate my health timeline that I realised something eye-opening.

It started when I was 12 and hospitalised with severe salmonella food poisoning – I lost a terrific amount of weight and had to be put on an IV drip. I was diagnosed with endometriosis in my thirties, followed by laparoscopy (keyhole surgery), fertility issues, multiple rounds of IVF, and miscarriages. There was a hip and spine injury that happened while I was filming, and a triple hernia operation two years prior to my breast cancer diagnosis . . . Looking at this timeline objectively I realised that this is a body that has been through some trauma – not to mention the three natural childbirths, one being the 'double bubble experience' of giving birth to twins. Of course, when you are through something, you tend to diminish or forget about it.

I didn't process any of these events properly when they happened. I failed to do any proper rehab after some of my major surgeries. I didn't protect myself against the onslaught of drugs I took when I was going through IVF. I didn't consider my gut microbiome when I was gulping down all the antibiotics I'd been prescribed. (I didn't even know what the gut microbiome *was* at that point.)

And I hadn't ever acknowledged the emotional pain of this medical history.

A chance discovery

I discovered a lump in my left breast while I was away filming in Costa Rica, back in the early months of 2020. When I returned to the UK, the world was spinning on a new axis of lockdowns and contagion amid the Covid-19 pandemic. I managed to get an appointment at a weirdly empty clinic and heaved a huge sigh of relief – through my face mask, then mandatory – when I was told the mass I'd found was just a benign group of microcysts.

'Keep an eye on it and come back in a year,' I was instructed.

I strolled out of the surgery and got on with my life. Twelve months later, in July 2021, I strolled back in for a routine check-up.

And then.

Although I'd had a local anaesthetic, I could feel the heavy, cold metal tool thumping into the flesh on the side of my breast. The noise reminded me of a machine we'd used in motor vehicle maintenance at school in Sheffield. I looked at it to put my mind at rest, and then wished I hadn't – it resembled the professional fabric hole punch my mum had used for leather belts in the design studio behind her shop.

Tears trickled down my face as I tried to control my breathing. I thought of my three young children. 'I want to watch them grow up,' I said to myself. 'I want to see who they become.'

A mammogram had shown nothing sinister, but I'd been sent for a 'just in case' ultrasound because my lump had become increasingly tender. The consultant and I were chatting about our respective summer holidays when he suddenly paused and exhaled, and in that second, I knew he'd found something untoward.

I could see what he could see on the ultrasound screen. It was just a tiny, dark pinprick, but it was enough to make the world as I knew it fall away.

Within a day, I found myself having the biopsy that felt as if someone was drilling into my breast.

The results came in a phone call the following week. Those benign microcysts had turned out to be a 6cm cancerous tumour. It was a large, high-grade tumour that could be trouble to treat. I was told I'd have to have it surgically removed, along with my left breast.

I have never been so afraid, so uncertain of the future, and so bewildered by what was happening.

The grief began almost immediately: grief for my health lost in an instant, grief for my life as I had known it, grief for that naive belief that I was invincible and everything was always going to be all right.

The reality is, when you hear the words 'You've got cancer,' you think you are going to die.

It's such a cliché, isn't it? To believe that you are beyond disease, to think that you'll never be the 'one' in that 'one in seven women' statistic (one in seven women develops breast cancer at some stage of their life). To assume that this could never happen to you.

In the weeks leading up to the operation, I was even more bereft; I didn't know what to do with my feelings of uncontrollable sadness, and I was baffled by the volume of unexpected tears at random intervals. I tried not to show my children my fear; telling them 'Mummy has cancer' was one of the hardest things I have ever had to do.

'Can we still hug you?' one of my little girls asked me.

The day before my surgery in October 2021, I took the advice of a friend, a doctor, who'd had a double mastectomy. She told me to say a formal farewell to my breast, so I thanked it for all its years of service: the breastfeeding, the bikinis, the jiggling about when I was running during sport. I'm glad I did, because acknowledging what I was about to go through, facing it head-on, turned out to be one of the things that helped me heal afterwards.

That was also when I promised myself I'd get outside every day of my life from then on. I would never let another morning or afternoon slide by without time in nature, being too busy to appreciate it and benefit from its multifaceted goodness.

When I got home from hospital five days later, I ensured I did my first rehabilitation exercises sitting in my garden, where I used the power of daylight and nature to recharge me. And every day thereafter, even at my most wobbly and grim, I insisted on a shuffle around outside, even if it was only for a few minutes.

I needed to see the sky and breathe some fresh air. I needed my London plane tree – I just didn't know it yet.

Soon, I started a simple exercise regime, shrugging my shoulders and spider-crawling my hand up a wall and over my head. One exercise involved lying on my back, putting my hands together in prayer and then touching the ground behind me. I thought I'd never be able to do that again. It took me four weeks of trying, and the joy when I succeeded was so intense I can still feel it today.

What I found the hardest – impossible, for a while – was looking at myself so horribly damaged.

It took until nearly Christmas before my Mama Mou could coax me into examining myself in a full-length mirror. I was making a documentary about my breast cancer (ITV's *Julia Bradbury: Breast Cancer and Me*) and I decided to do it on film. I remember turning to the camera and saying, 'It was always a career no, getting my breasts out on television, but here I go . . .'

That was eight weeks post-mastectomy. My nipple had been saved and my left breast had been reconstructed with a silicone prosthetic, but it was still scarred, swollen and angry.

Several weeks later, my mum examined it again. She looked up at me and said, 'Julia, it is beautiful . . .' I realised she was right.

* * *

We all deal with trauma in different ways, but I think one of the most important things you can do is to accept it as best you can. Own it. Figure out a way to go on. And make sure you ask other people to help you. I could not have handled my diagnosis, mastectomy and recovery without the love and support of my partner, my parents, my friends and my big sister Gina.

The other crucial thing to remember is that Mother Nature will be both your guardian and your guide. It's why every morning, I look out of my window at 'my' London plane tree and remember we can all regenerate, no matter how hostile our environment.

Walking is man's best medicine

Hippocrates said that – and he was right. Regular and longer walks have numerous benefits:

Two minutes in you begin to offset the harmful effects of sitting at your desk for an hour. You need to do these short walks multiple times a day and a minimum of two minutes of walking is recommended for every 30 minutes of sitting.

Five minutes in you have helped reset your circadian rhythm and improved your mood (but of course, if you have read the chapter on sleep, you'll already have done that by catching the morning light when you woke up).

Fifteen minutes in sugary cravings will be reduced – making you less likely to reach for high-calorie snacks. One study showed that participants ate fifty per cent less chocolate after a walk!

Sixty minutes in aids weight loss and staves off diabetes by helping bring your blood glucose under control.

Three minutes in your cardio-respiratory system activity increases, along with your heart rate. This increases the supply of blood to the brain.

Ten minutes in is long enough to increase (good) stress in your body, which triggers an overall anti-inflammatory stress-reducing response, post-exercise, and your creative thinking starts to improve.

Twenty minutes in your immune function is boosted with proven benefits in the cold and flu season.

Ninety minutes in reduces your risk of all-cause mortality – the catch is you have to do it every day to get the maximum benefit!

Healing and social fitness

As much as I have tried not to make *Walk Yourself Happy* a book about cancer, my diagnosis and having a mastectomy have undoubtedly created the biggest crisis of my life. The ripple effect on my partner, our three children, and the rest of my family, friends and brilliant colleagues has forever changed the way I see and interact with the world around me.

Psychotherapist Janet Reibstein, professor emerita at the University of Exeter's School of Psychology, is an expert in building better relationships with loved ones and the wider world. Her famous fans include Gwyneth Paltrow, Kirsty Young and Claudia Winkleman, and you might want to join them in reading her most recent book, *Good Relations: Cracking the code of how to get on better.*

Janet is a breast cancer survivor too, having had an elective double mastectomy back in the 1990s to save her from the disease, which had taken a woman from every generation of her family, including her mother and two maternal aunts.

It was a pioneering operation in that era, a brave and lonely thing to have to undergo.

Janet's past – living through the loss of her breasts and facing the ongoing threat of her cancer coming back – that's my future.

She is a stunning, strikingly beautiful woman. With a swag of silver hair, cat-like eyes and a bold fashion sense, you could imagine her striding along the Left Bank in Paris. Yet, at the time of our interview, she had just celebrated her seventy-sixth birthday. She's a mother and grandmother, and a clinician still at the peak of her career.

I wanted to know how she'd healed from breast cancer and gone on to enjoy her life without hesitation, setting aside grief and fear.

It turns out that, like me, Janet had made a promise to herself that she would live differently after cancer.

She bought herself an exercise bike to improve her physical fitness and began to walk wherever and whenever she could.

To protect her mental health, she dealt with toxic relationships, and ended one old friendship. 'I looked out for what was healthier for me, instead of cultivating things where there might be a question mark. Coming back from cancer made me sharper and smarter about relationships,' she says.

The next step was to improve every one of her interactions with both loved ones and strangers. She calls this 'social fitness', by which she means having the ability to relate well to other people, not just for their sake, but for your own, too.

She tells me: 'If you can learn a set of key communication skills, you will be improving your health and well-being as much as if you'd stopped smoking and gone on a healthy diet. More than anything, it's successful relationships of all kinds that lead to a happy, healthy life. A good social network can contribute to lower blood pressure and a lower incidence of obesity as well as better emotional well-being.

'Imagine having the confidence to get on with anyone. It's a skill that's likely to improve love, friendships, your family and your work. If you get those things right, if you are relationally capable, then you're winning at life.'

These are the four skills Janet says we all need to learn to achieve social fitness.

Emotional management: This is the ability to calm yourself when you begin to become emotional; when you are tense, ruffled, upset or angry.

Mentalising: This is placing yourself in the other person's position and feeling for them, but also understanding them as different from you.

Collaborative communication: This is making sure that your communication is clear and concise, and phrasing things in order to invite people to think along with you.

Making repairs: This is putting things back on track, including apologising when there's been hurt or upset, and also rewinding communications when there's been a break in understanding, to ensure you understand each other again.

A conversation with Janet Reibstein

Tell me about social fitness

Janet: There's a growing body of research that says social fitness is just as good as physical fitness and mental fitness in terms of well-being. It's actually a bedrock of wellness – if you get relationships right, you are more likely to be healthier, wealthier and wise. I'm not suggesting you use other people exploitatively. There needs to be give and take. The point is, it's a skill you can learn and then use to achieve a better outcome for both sides.

Is that with everybody you meet?

Janet: Absolutely. Even small encounters with people in the supermarket are a win in terms of social fitness. The more you can get people on your side, the more it becomes habitual to do that, and the better you get at it. View the small exchanges as training for the bigger ones. Similarly, the worse your everyday encounters, the more you're adding to the 'bank' of bad things for you and your body.

Does talking to my favourite London plane tree count?

Janet: Mmm, yes, I suppose so! Having a gratifying exchange gives you a gratifying experience. It adds to your 'bank' of good things.

Does a connection to nature count in terms of social fitness?

Janet: Yes, it does, though there is a hierarchy. Intimate relationships are the most important, but the wider and better your network, the better for you. (Within reason – having too many 'friends' probably means you don't have enough close and emotionally affecting ones.) We get meaning from all our relationships; usually these are with other people, but meaning could also be found by engaging with nature in a positive way.

And where do we start?

Janet: The first step has to be you. You take responsibility. People make the mistake of thinking that understanding must come from others – you're waiting for them to understand how something feels for you. It might be helpful to use mentalisation to think about how it might be impacting on the other person, too. If it's an interactional situation in a family, or between two people, there are *always* two parts to it. Acknowledge that with your language: 'There's an issue. It might be this or it might be that. I could be wrong. This is how it's impacting me. I'm wondering if this is what could be going on for you.' You're owning your own position, without blame. You might want to apportion blame; most people do. But instead, you're asking, 'What's the position for you, what's the feeling for you?' And that gives you a starting point for some sort of mutuality, some sort of understanding.

What if I think I already know how someone feels?

Janet: It's harder to deal with somebody you know very well, because you have built up, sometimes very wrongly, a whole set of assumptions about them. You come with a hypothesis about what this must be like for them, but you should be open-minded and inquisitive and not hold on to your hypothesis as a truth. It's harder to offend people you don't know well because they know you don't know them.

How do we ask for help from others?

Janet: You need to confront your fear and ask yourself, what is really scaring you here? What is the worst thing that can happen? Is that worse than what you're feeling now? Maybe you will be rejected. Not everybody will come through for you. You have to learn to take the risk. However, I think if you are socially fit, you have this general sense that the world will meet you on your terms, and that yes, help will be there.

How does walking help heal relationships?

Janet: It's like saying, 'Let's get some air.' Going out, looking at a lovely view, being in nature – it's a truism that [these things offer] a fresh start and a sense of perspective. The worst time to have an altercation is in a car with nowhere to go. You want to get out, but you can only lean in further. Bringing up difficult topics face to face is very hard. It's often a lot easier to walk alongside one another and focus on what's ahead of you. Whether you're aware of it or not, nature will be giving back to you.

Healing is such an individual response I thought this was the right chapter to share three inspirational stories in a row. You can read them now.

Mike's story: Walking to recovery

Mike Parry is a radio and television broadcaster who walked his way off the heart transplant list. His inspiration was the thousands of letters he received from fans of his shows on talk-SPORT (the world's biggest sports radio station). Initially, his goal was to walk the 200 yards to his local post box so he could reply to them.

Three years later, he completed the Great North Run – walking the half marathon course – and was met at the finishing line by British long-distance champion Paula Radcliffe.

It was 2004 when Mike almost died on a football job, covering the European Championships in Portugal. He was already ill and a combination of the heat and extreme hard work pushed him to breaking point. He likes to joke that Wayne Rooney saved his life, because the Everton star broke a toe and England went out of the tournament in the quarter finals. This early exit encouraged Mike to come home, too. Helped off the plane, the broadcaster was taken straight to hospital and diagnosed with acute heart failure.

He was so breathless, he couldn't walk down the street. Climbing the two flights of stairs to his apartment with a bag of groceries took him ten minutes and several stops. Standing five feet eight inches tall, he weighed twenty stones, much of it fluid that had accumulated in his lungs because of his failing heart. He would spend the next five months in and out of hospital, waiting for a donor heart, his life in the balance, his broadcasting career on hold and his anxiety overwhelming.

His whole life was dominated by the countdown to the call which would tell him a donor heart was available. He couldn't broadcast in case it came when he was live on air. Besides, by then he was so ill, he was barely able to leave home.

That's when he decided to get out and start walking.

'On my first try, I only got a hundred yards down the road before I had to have a sit on the wall and then go back,' he remembers. 'It took me three days just to get to the postbox, and I remember being absolutely elated. As the weeks passed, I'd take longer and longer routes, and eventually I was walking one mile, then two miles, then three. Soon, I was covering five or six miles a day in the North Downs. My life was transformed.

'Generally speaking, hearts do not repair themselves, but mine recovered, which is a very, very rare phenomenon. I walked myself back to normality.'

Mike suffers from dilated cardiomyopathy, in which the heart becomes enlarged and can't pump blood effectively. He describes his as looking like 'a flabby balloon'. It's most likely a genetic inheritance from his father, who died of heart failure at fifty-eight.

The broadcaster set himself a target of walking thirty miles a week, which led to him losing almost five stones in weight. In 2007, when he did the Great North Run in Newcastle upon Tyne, he was fitter and happier than he had been for years.

'Without a shadow of a doubt, I had gone against the medical orthodoxy, which was to be in bed, resting. When I said I wanted to walk, no one gave me a chance – apart from my own consultant.'

Two decades on, now aged sixty-eight, Mike still walks from his house to the station instead of taking the bus, and walks between appointments in London instead of catching the tube.

'It's always my first option,' he says, 'never my second. There's that sense of physical well-being. With every step I take, I feel a spring in my body, as though all my limbs are being regenerated. There are so many mental benefits, too. I do my best thinking when I walk. All my best ideas come to me like that. Walking completely sanitises your mind. It's like yoga or meditation; you just put one foot in front of the other and keep going, knowing you can't really come to any harm. It's quite magical.'

During his recovery, Mike bought a bike. 'It was a jolly expensive one,' he recalls, 'but I hated it. I abandoned it in the car park under my flat, and I think someone stole it. I hadn't looked at it or thought about it for so long that I have no idea when it disappeared. I just walk.'

Stronger than we imagine

Many people, like Mike Parry, like Janet, like me, have come back from serious illness. There are others who live with it every day, never knowing when it will strike and cleave them from their families, their work and their independence. Anne Welsh, an author, entrepreneur and philanthropist is one of them.

I'm going to tell her story here because she has made it her mission in life to help others in a similar situation, through her health platform Painless Universal.

Anne was born with sickle cell disease, which she feared would bar her from motherhood and her chosen career in the heavy-weight world of investment banking. It did neither. Today, she runs her own consultancy firm in London, is a mother of two, and campaigns internationally to raise awareness.

Sickle cell disease is an inherited blood disorder in which red blood cells, which are normally disc-shaped, are crescent- or 'sickle'-shaped. These cells do not bend or move easily, and can block blood flow to the rest of the body. This leads to a cascade of health problems, including strokes and infections, and episodes of extreme pain. For Anne, these were so acute that paramedics sent to take her to hospital couldn't touch her body without administering morphine.

She was just three years old when she was diagnosed at Great Ormond Street Hospital, and by the time she was twenty-eight, Anne was wondering why she was still alive.

'My body was a death sentence,' she says, frankly. 'I was speaking to my mentor and I said, "I think this is the day I'm done; I don't want to go ahead, not with my life like this."'

Gently, he reminded her she had a loving family, a roof over her head, food on her plate, and top-quality medical care. Some sickle cell disease sufferers in developing countries have none of those things. (More than seventy per cent of people around the world with sickle cell disease live in Africa.)

For Anne, it was a transformative conversation, reminding her she was so focused on the bad times that she never celebrated the good. She would eventually write a book, *Pain-less*, part memoir and part self-help book, about this understanding, and people responded to it in their thousands – not just those with sickle cell disease, but anyone living with chronic pain.

She had found her audience. She had found people in whom joy sparked despite their illness, and sometimes because of it.

Today, she addresses millions globally and her message is always the same: 'We are stronger than we imagine, all of us. You don't know how strong you can be until strong is the only way out.'

Pain, she says, is just something you go through, a bad spot on a long journey, like turbulence on a plane. 'We need to persevere, to fight, to find our will to get through and have the life we want.'

Anne's success has been achieved through iron discipline, her supremely stylish sense of self, and walking, something she knows is often a challenge for people living with chronic pain. 'Lifestyle changes are the biggest fear we have,' she admits. 'Because when you try something new, you're scared you're just going to add to your pain . . . Go outside and walk more, I mean, why would you risk it?'

On medical advice, though, she did.

It started after she'd had her daughter (five at the time of writing) by Caesarean section. Anne ended up in intensive care with the kind of complications that are all too normal for someone with sickle cell disease. Her pain was extreme.

She asked for a wheelchair so she could go and see her new daughter, but a doctor encouraged her to walk instead.

'Just try to take baby steps,' he told her.

'My first thought was, "Haven't you seen my condition? Why would you want me to do that?!"' remembers Anne. 'I was very, very disheartened because I felt so tired. My blood pressure was low and not rising. My oxygen saturation levels were low because of all the morphine I'd been taking. My breathing wasn't great. My leg was swollen.

'But my doctor said, "Anne, just walk a little bit. I need to see your heart pumping. I don't need you to run; I do need you to challenge your body."

'I committed to doing it every day and then twice a day, starting with a walk down the corridor and up a flight of stairs. Within a week, I was doing two flights. I noticed my recovery speeding up. I was healing faster and better – and, of course, I had the brilliant motivation of my new baby.

'When you have a chronic illness and you are asked to walk, all you think about is pain, pain, pain, but sometimes exercise does not bring pain – it brings joy. I soon realised that by walking more, I'd be fighting all kinds of things rather than just playing doormat to my disease.'

Today, Anne still walks. She parks her car as far away as possible from her many business meetings, and wears smart trainers or comfortable shoes, with a pair of her signature designer high heels stowed in her handbag.

'I'm obsessed with walking,' she admits. 'It's the biggest deal for me. I understand why people might be frightened of the gym because you can easily hurt yourself in there, but with walking, there is no risk. Nothing. You just wrap up if it's rainy and go for it. Every time I head out, it's like being in a new world, where the air smells better and I listen to the birds and nursery children in the park, and I notice the happiness it sparks in me. I couldn't live without it now.

'I mean, what is the alternative? Being stuck on a treadmill which is killing you; fall off, climb back on again, more pain. Walking might look like it's going to be hard – and perhaps it will be in the first week. But by the second and third week, it's no longer pain, it's a gain.

'So get outdoors! Honestly, it's the best medicine there is.'

 ## Charlie's story: Birdsong

Charlie Corbett should have known more about birds. He grew up on farms on the Wessex Downs and the Isle of Mull, and lived according to nature's calendar. But what he'd learned about ornithology as a child was forgotten during his two decades working as a financial journalist in London.

It would take a family tragedy for him to rediscover it.

Charlie's mother was diagnosed with a brain tumour aged just sixty-six. Lying grief-stricken on a hill in the rain near his Wiltshire family home, he heard a skylark. Its distinctive song transported him, reminding him of the beauty and power of the natural world, a promise that life would go on.

'It was like an injection of neat hope,' he says.

When his mother died six months later, Charlie found comfort in the sound of a song thrush singing at the end of a long, dark night, and the trilling of a wren, which he calls the Dolly Parton of the bird world: 'Small, gutsy and with a voice that can be heard in three counties.'

The sight of acrobatic house martins arriving from Africa in the spring cheered him. So, too, did the electric blue and burnished orange flash of a kingfisher flying Spitfire-fast over a river. He woke to blackbirds serenading the sunrise and found his nights soothed by the hooting of a tawny owl.

After a year of plugging in to this surround-sound of bird-song, he wrote a book about it, *12 Birds to Save Your Life*.

Over the last decade – his mum died in 2012 – Charlie has immersed himself in the world of birds while maintaining his career as an executive coach and speaker in banking and finance. When I caught up with him, he was heading to Boston on a business trip.

'Right now, I'm trapped in Heathrow Terminal Five, but standing in my garden this morning, I heard a chiffchaff sing and realised this little thing, which weighs less than an ounce, had flown a similar number of miles as I'm about to – four thousand – from North Africa to get to an English oak.

'With birds, there's always something going on just outside your back door, whether it's a treecreeper nesting at the side of your shed, a naughty magpie stealing some eggs, or corn buntings cruising across a field in search of insects.

'I saw my first swallow the other day and it was thrilling, the harbinger of summer. Come autumn, there'll be great waves of winter birds coming down from the north: brent geese, barnacle geese, whooper swans sweeping in from Iceland. Tuning in to all this birdlife reminds us we are of this planet, we're not just here looking at it.

'I think sometimes we behave like an alien species that's been randomly dropped off – we have dislocated ourselves from nature and it's not good for us. We watch, but we don't see. We listen, but we don't hear. We treat the natural world like some old, fading wallpaper – it's there, but we don't notice it anymore.

'Previous generations were closer to it than we are, and it made them better able to cope with anxiety, death and change. They understood that life is part of a vast cycle. Birds and bird-song, all of nature, is such a powerful metaphor for that.

'If I go a few days without taking stock of my surroundings, I'm a sad human being. The answer is to step outside and adminis-ter some of my own medicine – to listen to the birds.'

This chapter is about hope as much as healing, and being confi-dent that the strength you need to cope with an ailment or a crisis is already there within you. It's also about knowing that nature models resilience and regeneration to us in the toughest of times.

I see both of those things when I look at my lovely London plane tree. Creamy young bark underneath. Tougher old olive-coloured bark on top. Long, graceful catkins dangling down. Those thick, leathery maple-shaped leaves, vivid green in spring, a rich orange in autumn, carving their patterns on the city skyline.

London planes: they're the canopy on the Mall, they're where a nightingale sang in Berkeley Square, they're your shade when you take a sunny walk along the bank of the Thames. You'll find them all over the world, too, from New York to Johannesburg to Sydney. They are strong and beautiful and heal themselves again and again, helping other living things across the long span of their lives.

Sue's seeds of wisdom on healing

Adapting to any form of significant loss is a complex process. Somehow, we have to find a way to accept a new and unwelcome reality. We encounter many different kinds of loss in the course of our lives, but those that involve our health or work or close relationships can be particularly difficult to adjust to.

At times when we feel stuck and unable to see a way forward, talking can help, but walking is also useful, because getting the body moving seems to help us process emotions and thoughts. The sixteenth-century philosopher Montaigne understood this aspect of the mind–body connection from personal experience. As he put it: 'My mind will not budge unless my legs move it.'

Furthermore, in times of crisis, nature's powers of regeneration can be very sustaining to us. Through observing seasonal changes, we are able to connect with the cycle of life, in which destruction and decay are followed by regrowth and renewal.

You may notice these things spontaneously, but if not, you need to intentionally focus on them as you walk. Look out for signs of new life springing up from the earth, as well as buds on the trees or any fruits that are forming. Different seasons will offer different experiences, but even in winter there will be signs of growth somewhere.

The American psychiatrist Robert Lifton thought that in order to face major loss, we need access to a form of what he called 'symbolic survival'. One of the most powerful forms of this is the consolation we can experience through the continuity of nature. As a result, many people find at times of crisis that their relationship with nature takes on a whole new significance.

7

Fancy Feet

*'The human foot is a masterpiece of
engineering – and a work of art.'*
Leonardo da Vinci

The good news is that I can touch my toes. The bad news is that I don't want to. I've inherited my dad's feet, and I'm sorry to say they ain't pretty. They're long, spindly size sevens, and after the birth of my twin girls, I started to develop another inherited trait: a bunion. Thanks, Dad.

It's a shame, because I like feet. I notice other people's. I'm definitely a foot person. My mother and sister both have beautiful almond-shaped trotters with perfect toenails, and I particularly loved my babies' feet when they were newborn – all those sweet little sausage toes just waiting to be tickled.

I made my own feet a lot worse with a textbook mistake shortly after my girls arrived. I started to film a new walking series, and did the entire thing in box-fresh hiking boots, contrary to the advice I *always* give everyone else: never ever use new boots for long walks. Make sure you 'break them in' first.

This pair was exceptionally comfortable, but they had a sealed ankle feature; great for riverbanks and soggy terrain but so well insulated my feet were endlessly hot and sweaty. Soon, my feet were as soft and squidgy as those of my six-month-old babies

– added to which, they had yet to recover from the pressures of a twin pregnancy.

Being me, I kept pounding on up the hills and along the trails of the UK. By the end of every day, my dogs were barking. (I love this way of saying I had sore feet, but in case it's new to you, it was apparently coined in 1913 by a journalist writing in the *New York Evening Journal*. It may have been picked up from the cockney rhyming slang 'dog meat – feet', but it was popularised by US servicemen, who exported it globally in World War Two. You're welcome.)

Apart from blisters, I'd never had a foot problem before. Now, after filming ended, I ended up consulting a specialist who diagnosed a painful case of plantar fasciitis. At one stage, it was so sore I had to have a steroid injection on the bony tops of my feet, right between my toes. Then I was ordered to begin a dedicated foot exercise programme. 'Something else to take care of as my body slowly declines into older age,' I thought.

Prior to this, my idea of foot care had been a luxurious pedicure, so actually it was a blessing in disguise because it meant I had to take my feet more seriously. I'm glad I did, and I'd urge you to start, because they deserve it. They support the entire body, keep us mobile, and allow us to get out into nature and do many of the things we want and need to do.

Examine them closely, and you'll find a superhighway of blood vessels and nerves, muscles and ligaments, with a skeletal system so intricate it poses challenges for the scientists who try to map it. That's right – we're still puzzling over how to make computer and robotic models of the human foot, restricting our understanding of how we move.

Isn't that incredible? Mother Nature has designed feet so brilliantly, we don't yet know all there is to know about them. Feet are a feat of evolutionary engineering to match any other part of your body.

However, they're also one of the most overlooked (really) body parts when it comes to general health. How many of you do foot and ankle exercises when you're at the gym? (Hmmm, thought not.) Yet our feet are the foundation of our bodies in terms of support, balance, posture, and overall wellbeing.

You probably know a friend or family member who has fallen or slipped while doing something relatively mundane, like walking up or down the stairs, or navigating a pavement. I know I've been a bit of a doom-monger in some chapters of this book, but I'm afraid I have another disheartening fact for you: globally, an estimated 684,000 fatal falls occur each year, making it the second leading cause of unintentional injury death after road traffic accidents. Around the world, death rates from falls are highest among adults over the age of sixty, according to the World Health Organization.[1]

Even if a nasty fall doesn't kill you, approximately 37.3 million of them are severe enough every year for people to need ongoing medical attention. People who fall and suffer a disability, particularly the older generation, are at major risk of requiring subsequent long-term care and institutionalisation.

Sadly, I think we all know of an elderly relative with a broken hip who has never fully recovered. (If a broken hip is not quickly and correctly treated, there's a thirty to forty per cent chance an older patient will die within a year.) A fall can be the beginning of the end, which is why staying mobile (walking), strong (see Chapter 8) and taking care of all our body parts, including feet, is vital for health span.

Keeping your feet happy

I turned to Helen Branthwaite PhD to find out more about feet. She trained as a podiatrist and is now a senior lecturer in clinical biomechanics (human movement) at Staffordshire University's School of Health, Science and Wellbeing. She has a masters in sports injuries and her PhD examined the effects of everyday footwear on our movement. She's the person who advised

Parliament on the effect of wearing high heels when there were calls for a ban on them being mandatory in some roles, such as for receptionists and airline cabin crew.

At parties, Helen usually dodges questions about what branch of healthcare she practises. When she tells people it's feet, they either recoil or take their socks off and ask her to have a look at their ingrown toenails (seriously). Sometimes she says she is a podiatrist and awaits the customary response: 'Ah, so you work with children.'

Helen doesn't mind this, but it does reveal a lot about how much time and thought we give our feet. However, if you want to walk to stay well, you're going to have to make like Leonardo and start seeing feet as miraculous.

Helen loves hers. They are strong and supple, and a size six, which is the average for a British woman. You're most likely to find her in Havaiana flip-flops, which she busts out the minute spring comes. (She can walk for miles in them, though that doesn't go for most of us – she always sees an upsurge in podiatry cases after the first sunny weekend of the year.) The foot expert is a fan of high heels, too, just as long as she's only going from taxi to restaurant and back.

'It doesn't matter what you wear for an evening out,' she says, 'as long as, you know, you don't fall over.'

So that's two foot myths busted by the woman who advises the Royal College of Podiatry on walking: flip-flops can be good for your feet because they demand a wide range of movements to keep you stable, and you can still love your Louboutins, just not every day.

Actually, any shoe that demands your feet do something different – including heels or flip-flops – is beneficial, says Helen. If you always wear cool trainers, you're not doing your feet any favours, because they'll become they *only* thing you can wear.

Around twenty per cent of the population will have a foot injury or chronic problem that prevents them from walking normally at some point in their life.[2] It might be short term, but foot pain and dysfunction can result in permanent disability. The miraculous thing about feet, though, is that often the solution is instantaneous. 'Stop wearing the wrong shoes, or even the wrong socks, and you're better,' says Helen.

Recently, Helen worked with a lady in her eighties whose painful feet were curbing her ability to get out with her dog.

'I asked her to bring in her dog-walking shoes, and she brought in a beautiful pair of patent pumps with a little Cuban heel, a bit like Queen Elizabeth used to wear,' remembers Helen. 'I told her she needed trainers. Cushioned soles. Better grip. She didn't want to try them; she thought they were for the younger generation. I convinced her, and now I pass her out walking every day, still with her dog, chatting to everyone. As well as preserving her walking, paying attention to her feet has helped her maintain her social life and her place in the community.'

This woman had what Helen calls health literacy – she was willing to learn about her own health and make changes to preserve the function of her feet. At the other end of the spectrum was a much younger client, a high-earning business executive in her thirties with chronic pain at the front of her foot. She was in despair, having done the rounds of her GP, a hospital consultant, and a physio in search of a cure for the issue, which was also starting to hurt her knees and hips. When Helen asked her to bring in her everyday shoes, she proudly arrived with a case of beautiful Chanel and Manolo Blahnik six-inch stilettos, and the kind of plain but tall heels from L.K. Bennett favoured by Catherine, Princess of Wales.

Helen, a blunt-speaking Mancunian, told her patient the shoes were destroying her feet. It's not that high heels are inherently wrong, but their tight, shallow toe boxes (the technical name for the bit of the shoe that houses your tootsies) were very, very wrong for this patient's particular feet. 'She refused point blank to accept there was nothing I could do, no insert I could make, that would keep her in them,' says Helen. 'She said she wasn't stopping, not for anything, because they were part of her identity. I told her I'd see her after she'd had surgery, because that was where she was headed.

'I'm not against pretty shoes – I love them, and I recently made orthotics for another patient who was a salsa dancer. Her dancing shoes weren't for everyday use, and weren't going to destroy her feet. That's the difference. Shoes are an important factor in self-image and how we portray ourselves to the rest of the world. Take a white trainer with red laces and a flash of leopard print. Sizzling. Take the same trainer in a dull navy with a grubby grey lace? Orthopaedic.

'The point is, you have tons of choice these days, and the key is to choose footwear that is fit for purpose, especially if it's for a walk.'

It's safe to say the study of walking and keeping your feet fit enough to do it well is Helen's 'thing', and she's got a quarter of a century of caring for other people's feet behind her. You want her top tip for happy feet? Two or three short exercises to be done daily (see pages 188–9), and a mini-massage.

'Sore feet aren't like having a bad back,' Helen points out. 'You can actually reach your own feet!'

Finally, you have to lavish them with cream containing urea – yes, the same stuff that's in your pee. (The old military tradition of soldiers weeing in their boots to break them in and protect the skin on their feet? A bit stinky but it worked, confirms Helen.)

A conversation with Helen Branthwaite

What is walking?

Helen: Walking is a habitual pattern of complex movements that we learn to get us from A to B. Whether it's rising from a chair to go to the kitchen for a cuppa, or trekking across the Scottish Highlands, it's the first choice of movement for humans. There's a lot to perfect: bones, nerves, muscles and tendons, all coming together to refine an action which is so fundamental to us we see it as our right, rather than a privilege.

As a species, we have evolved to move on two limbs. It's pretty inefficient compared to a cheetah, say, but being up on two legs helped early man reach and grab things and, when we were hunting, to throw stones and spears. We've adapted to lots of different environments down the centuries, and are still capable of doing so. Today, humans spend a lot of time walking on very hard floors, creating repetitive wearing movements that early man did not endure. Yet we manage just fine, and most of us go through life without any problems walking.

Tell me about foot structure

Helen: There are fifty-two main bones in both of your feet combined, which is a quarter of the total number of bones in your body. These bones are held together with a complex network of ligaments and connective tissue, with thirty-three joints in each foot. The joints are responsible for movement, shock absorption and creating rigidity. Attached to the bones are the tendon muscle units, with over one hundred separate muscles controlling activity in the foot.

On average, your foot is the length of your forearm, which in turn is as wide as your pelvis. It grows rapidly from birth to your teens and stops completely at the age of twenty. Its dimensions are all linked, from the shape of your arch to the height of your foot, as well as the length. These are the measurements used in the manufacture of all footwear, from hiking boots to killer heels.[3] As we age, the integrity and structure of the bones in your feet alter, especially if you are a woman heading into menopause. This can change foot length and shape, resulting in an entirely different foot structure to the one you previously had. What I'm saying is, don't be surprised if you suddenly start taking a different shoe size.

So what's going on in our feet when we walk?

Helen: In a normal stride, we start at what we call heel strike (where your heel hits the ground before the rest of your foot), with a relatively straight leg and a flexed hip. We control our movement by rocking forward through the ankle joint, which brings the front part of the foot to the floor.

The synchronicity of these foot, knee and hip joints moving together absorbs the shock of hitting the ground and allows for controlled muscle contractions, shifting our body weight forward. During this phase, the knee will start to move over the toes so the heel lifts off the floor, like a spring. We are propelled on to the big toe, which then rocks us forward again.

Coupled with these movements are rotations in the pelvis, spine and arms. And all this is only for when we are walking in a straight line! You want me to talk about the challenge of a big hill or a slippery surface or a long distance – that's another chapter! We are constantly adapting while we are on the go to ensure we do not fall flat on our faces.

What's the most common foot problem we are likely to face?

Helen: The price your feet pay for many years on Earth is something called hallux rigidus, which is arthritis in the big toe joint. Athletes, footballers and runners often get it early, because it's a 'stubbing' injury. It's years in the making, and before it reaches the end stage, there's tons you can do – exercise and orthotics – to help. So, if you think you're getting it, go and see a podiatrist.

Like everything else about your feet, it's got consequences for the rest of your body. Losing the mechanism to propel yourself forward, as the toe joint stiffens and becomes unable to flex, poses a challenge to your knees, pelvis and spine. You compensate; either the foot twists towards the instep, creating increased pressure on the knee, or it twists towards the little toe, loading the lesser metatarsals or the ball of the foot. Do that often enough, and you have got issues way beyond the initial problem of an arthritic big toe.

Helen's favourite foot myths

Hallux rigidus is real, but honestly, there are so many myths about feet passed down from generation to generation. Often there's a really straightforward solution to a foot problem, meaning you can whisk off your socks and shoes in the summer without hesitation. Here's my list of favourites:

Myth	Fact
A corn grows with a centre which needs to be cut out for it to be treated.	A corn is a focal collection of hard skin that often forms in a conical shape over a bony notch. It is the result of increased force over a particular area. Removal will stop it hurting but won't cure it. The corn will reform if the underlying causes aren't addressed.
Bunions form because the shoes I wore as a child were too tight and pointy, or were passed down from a sibling.	Nope. The formation of bunions is not known to be caused by footwear. It is more likely to be a hereditary problem, where bone shape and length, joint flexibility and inherent muscle weakness are key factors. People around the world who do not regularly wear shoes get bunions too – and some people only develop the deformity in one foot. A bunion is often not painful or arthritic. Wearing shoes that are too tight around the joint might hurt, but it won't have caused the initial changes.

Flat feet are bad, and you need to get treatment.	Approximately five per cent of the population have flat feet – it's a normal variant of the human form. If you are born flat-footed (it is often hereditary), it will probably not cause you any problems. In fact, many elite athletes have flat feet. Getting a flat foot because of injury is different, as there is often trauma and damage to ligaments and tendons that can cause significant changes to the way you move. Then it's a problem.
Pain in the heel is always plantar fasciitis.	There are multiple causes of heel pain; plantar fasciitis is just one of them. People only talk about it because they've heard of it! The plantar fascia is a connective tissue in the heel that can sometimes tear and thicken, causing pain. Symptoms include pain on getting up and a reduction in symptoms when walking. What you think is plantar fasciitis could be a heel bone bruise, referred pain from your back, a reduction in the fat pad in your foot or an Achilles tendon problem.
Verrucas are caught in the swimming pool.	A verruca is a skin virus that usually appears on the sole of the foot. For you to catch one, there needs to be a break in the skin. You can pick up the virus from any communal bathing area including your family bathroom. Actually, there is a bit of truth in the swimming pool myth – the changing rooms and the poolside expose you to other people's bare feet, so it's a good idea to wear flip-flops to prevent spread.

These socks were made for walking

People have been wearing socks since the time of the ancient Egyptians, who wore socks with their sandals – which is either very fashion-forward or a real faux pas, depending on your taste. These socks were made from matted animal hair and had webbing for the big toe and the lesser toes. You might not think that sounds as though they have much in common with today's socks, but they served the same purpose: acting as an environmental control layer between our feet and our shoes.

In the twenty-first century, the material a sock is made from ensures the foot is either kept warm, by trapping air particles in between the layers, or kept cool, by wicking away excessive moisture from the foot (a good summer sock is there to limit the sweatiness of the foot).[4]

Choosing the correct sock for a walk is a very personal matter. What shoes will you be wearing? How far are you going? What's the temperature? How's the terrain? You have to consider all these things.

The styling and design of the sock is important, too, especially for longer walks and challenging hikes. Walking socks have been developed to include padding in the heel and around the toes. They've got dual layers to minimise friction and prevent blisters, and compression in the arch to give your foot a cuddle and keep a snug (but not too snug) fit.

Printed plastics on socks – by which I mean grippy socks and Pilates socks – can really help if your foot is slipping around inside your shoe, creating friction.

Helen says: 'A patient of mine who was planning a trek across Costa Rica came to ask my advice on socks, because she hadn't had a lot of luck with them in training. Any time she walked more than thirteen miles, she got burning and redness on the ball of her foot. She had been wearing Coolmax™ socks, which are a polyester blend of material designed to wick moisture away from the skin, because she knew it would be hot in Costa Rica.

'She was on the right track; that's a respected brand and would have been the perfect choice for many people. However, because of her individual foot shape, her socks were rubbing around the big toe joint when she walked. Her feet twisted inside her boots more than is usual. By changing to a grip sock, we were able to reduce the shearing forces under her foot, and immediately she could manage twenty miles without pain. She kept the Coolmax socks for shorter walks after that.'

Cotton socks are often a go-to when it's hot, as they tend to keep your foot cooler than a sock made from alternative natural fibres like bamboo. However, modern manufactured materials, like modal, will always allow for a hotter foot to have more air circulating around it. So, you might want to think about a man-made fabric on your feet, even if you wear cotton T-shirts or trousers. (I'm going to declare a personal preference here for natural fabrics and fibres. I'm not a fan of plastic-based materials for any type of clothing, especially if it's a material that is close to a sweaty part of you. Some materials have been treated with chemicals to create a particular look and feel, and the micro-plastics in these socks can shed their particles into the pores of your skin. Natural fibres are better for the planet, too, if they've been sustainably sourced. Bear in mind that 92 million tons of clothing end up in landfill every year.)

If you're going on a cold walk, look for a thick thermal sock, and don't stop until you have found one that reaches your knee.

Longer, rougher terrain might mean you'll benefit from dual layering to minimise friction, or grippy socks to limit stress on the foot. Work out whether you prefer padding in the heel or in your toes, or both.

The 'climate' of your foot inside your sock is very individual – only you know what feels comfortable, and it won't be the same as the people you are walking with. You'll have to experiment with different types to find out.

Walking boots and shoes

Here's Helen's advice for choosing walking boots and shoes.

Your choice of walking boots and shoes is dependent on terrain and distance – it's that simple. If I'm walking my cock-a-poo, May, over the fields, I'll be in wellies; if it's along the road, then it's my trusty trainers with their grippy soles every time. But if I'm on a day's hike, it'll be boots. What matters is that your footwear is fit for purpose.

If your walk is on a flat canal path, or along a pavement where the movements are repetitive and high impact, then you may want to wear a lightweight trainer with a cushioned sole. The weight of the shoe is significant in terms of how much energy you use. A heavy shoe hanging like a dead weight on the end of your leg uses up more energy during walking. Most modern running shoes are manufactured from lightweight foams and only weigh about 250g. The sole is constructed to improve shock absorbency and shaped to maximise function. The uppers are knitted and accommodate any joint protrusions, which limits irritation and pressure on the bony bits of your feet.

They're great for walking, but – and it's a big but – they might not have the stability you need for tougher terrain. Also, they can get very wet. Some models come with a Gore-Tex™ layer that resolves that problem, but be clear about what you want and need.

I'm a big fan of trail-running shoes. I think the name tends to put people off; they sound as if they're for serious cross-country runners, but they're a fantastic hybrid between a sturdy boot and a regular trainer. Check them out. Yet even they can be troublesome for walking if it's wet underfoot, because the grip on their soles might not be sufficient. Again, some makes have a more rugged sole, making them safer and more comfortable in damp weather, so do your research and shop around.

The benefit of choosing a proper walking shoe is that the sole has improved traction built in. This is better if you are walking off road, up hills, on rougher terrain and across grassy fields. The grip of the sole will hold you steady when the ground is slippery. The materials and tread pattern improve the friction between the ground and the shoe, ensuring your walk is enjoyable, not exhausting.

Holding yourself still and steady on a slippery surface in trainers creates a lot of hard work. Think about walking on icy roads or snowy paths. If there is not enough traction between the shoe and the surface, then your leg muscles have to work harder by contracting to stabilise the movements and hold you upright. Wearing a true walking shoe will help dodge that.

If your walk includes rocky climbs and undulating pathways, well, then, you'll want to upgrade all the way to a boot with additional support around the ankle. Having a supportive padded collar around the ankle stabilises the movement, meaning you are less likely to sprain your ankle. This is most useful if the ground is unpredictable or if the walk is going to last all day – the ankle support helps reduce muscle fatigue and gives you a little energy boost along the way.

In the depths of winter, or if you are lucky enough to be walking abroad in a mountainous region, consider adding reinforcements to your sole. Something like Yaktracks® clamp to the sole of the shoe and provide additional grip. They're easy to apply and universal fitting.

All of these suggestions give you an insurance policy against the falls and fractures I spoke about earlier in the chapter, which cost the NHS here in the UK billions every year.

Whatever shoe type you are looking to buy or wear, here are some rules from Helen to keep you comfortable.

1. Consider the weight of the shoe – remember, the lighter the better, without compromising on fit and structure.

2. The more shoe you have on your foot, the more support it's giving you. A full-ankle boot will be more rigid than a half-ankle boot, which will be more rigid than a shoe.

3. Look for a lacing system that can be loosened or threaded differently if there is foot swelling or a bony deformity. This means you can make more room in a shoe in the appropriate position. In the case of a bunion, avoid the lace hole around that area to give more room.

4. Ensure that the sole has an inclined angle so that the heel section is thicker than the sole at the front of the shoe. This 'wedged' design will enable your body weight to rock forward and limit the amount of work your ankle has to do (see figure 1).

5) Assess the stiffness of the sole. The more rigid the sole, the less work your foot will do and the more suited the shoe is to rough terrain. Mountaineering boots have solid soles with no flexion. Trainers can be 'wrung out'. Test a prospective purchase by gripping the sole and bending and twisting. If it collapses in your hands, then it generally will not help support the foot on a long walk in the hills (see figure 2).

Figure 1: The height of the shoe heel needs to be around 1cm higher than the front of the shoe so that there is an inclination to the arch, rather than being completely flat.

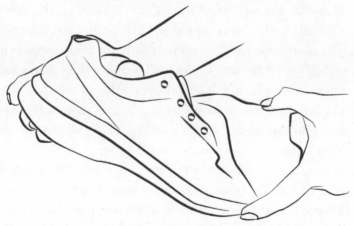

Figure 2: Twisting the shoe and flexing the toe give an estimate of how the sole of the shoe moves. This will help you decide if the shoe will support your foot. The stiffer the shoe, the more support you will get.

And do remember to go to a shop that sells multiple brands, not just one brand with different designs. Different brands use different lasts (the solid form around which a shoe is moulded), and you'll know when you try on the right one!

 ## Uggs and Crocs

We are lucky to live in an era when utilitarian shoes have crossed over into the everyday. Trainers, once the preserve of the sports field, are now a wardrobe staple for us all.

The Ugg boot was originally created for sheep shearers in Australia in the 1920s, and was then discovered by the country's surfers and adopted as cosy beachwear in the 1960s and 1970s. They went global at the turn of the millennium.

Crocs were first targeted at the sailing community: bold, comfy, grippy and unsinkable. The first production run of 200 pairs sold out at the 2001 Fort Lauderdale Boat Show, and the rest is history. US presidents, Hollywood royalty and even heirs to the throne (Prince George) have all been seen in them over the years, and they've been given quirky fashion cred by fans such as Kanye West, Ariana Grande, Justin Bieber and Nicki Minaj.

But you will not see me in Crocs. Ever. Ugly? I think so. Biodegradable? Not yet. They're currently made from ethylene-vinyl acetate, which remains in landfill or the oceans for decades. However, the plan is for Crocs to become 100 per cent plant based by 2030. (But don't try eating them!)

Exercising your feet

It's a lot to take in, given how little you think about your feet, isn't it?

However, there are huge mental and physical health benefits to be had from walking and being outdoors, and Helen sees a lot of sad, angry and frustrated patients whose pain or an injury is stopping them from enjoying these things. She thinks that walking is something many of us take for granted, and she's right, we do often take it for granted. What you have to remember is that walking is also a physically demanding activity, so if you are hurt or have something wrong with your feet, you need recovery and rehabilitation. If you fell and twisted your ankle while you were out running, you'd elevate it and use ice to bring down the swelling. Then you'd slowly return to walking as the pain subsided, before building up to a slow jog. You wouldn't attempt a proper run until you were back to fitness. But rehabilitation is so much harder when walking itself is the activity you want to do!

You can prevent many chronic problems by committing to an exercise regime for your feet. As we age, the strength of our muscles declines, with changes occurring from the age of forty.[5] The only way to ensure all our muscles maintain function and strength is to train them (see Chapter 8).

Your feet have loads of muscles in them, and they respond to training in the same way as your biceps and your abs. You wouldn't launch into a long wild swim in a cold lake without training, nor would you go on a cycling holiday without preparing. Look at the famous 'Couch to 5K' running plan – isn't it time there was something similar for walking?

Helen tells us that training your feet doesn't mean going out and doing more walking; it means specifically isolating particular muscles to build strength, grip and flex. You need to go up and down on your tiptoes, then flex your toes, extend them, and wiggle them as much as you can. Try picking up a sock from the bedroom floor with your feet, or invest in a proper therapy ball. (Therapy balls can be smooth or spiky and come in varying sizes. Rolled around under the feet, they stimulate blood flow, relieve tension and reduce pain in the foot area.)

Simple foot exercises

Here are diagrams of simple exercises that cover the range of movements you need in your feet. You can do some of them while cleaning your teeth, sitting at your desk or watching the TV.

Start standing up, with both feet flat on the ground in a relaxed position. Exercises 1 and 2 can be done with both feet at the same time.

1. Lift up the toes from the floor, keeping the ball of the foot pressed into the ground. Hold for two to three seconds, and return to the relaxed position. Initially, try to repeat five times, and then build the number of repetitions over time.

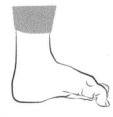

2. Scrunch the toes like a gripping fist, shortening the arch and grabbing with the toes. Having a sock or towel to grip will help in the first instance. Relax and return to starting position. Again, repeat five times, building up the repetitions.

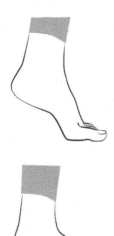

3. Elevate up on to the tiptoes as far as is comfortable and hold for two to three seconds, then lower to a hovering position, where you do not quite put your heel down. Repeat by going straight up to your toes again. Count how many repetitions you can do before feeling tightness and tiredness in the back of your leg. Write this down and check your progress against the table below, which shows the normal number of single-leg heel raises that each age group and sex should be able to complete. This is the target you should aim for if you can't already. Be progressive and slow in trying to get to the end goal.[6]

Age (years)	Number of heel lifts (male)	Number of heel lifts (female)
20	37	30
30	33	27
40	28	24
50	24	22
60	19	19
70	14	15
80	10	13

The importance of balance

Balance is a big thing in foot health because it's so connected to your broader physical well-being and your life expectancy.[7]

The Harvard Medical School says: 'The sense of balance typically worsens with age. Poor balance often leads to falls, which can cause serious head injuries and other disabling injuries. Hip fractures in particular can lead to serious health complications and threaten independence. A combination of activities such as walking, strength training and specific workouts can improve balance and prevent falls. Walking helps build lower-body strength, an important element of good balance.'[8]

Helen explains that our balance deteriorates as we get older because the nerve receptors in the foot – the things that tell you where you are in space – shrink with age. Stimulating them with exercises can help. She suggests standing on one leg, with support, to start with. Once you have mastered that, make the exercise more challenging by closing your eyes or bending forwards.

Eventually, you could work up to using a wobble cushion with a textured surface (the texture is designed to stimulate the nerve endings in your feet). If you are worried about trying this exercise, or have specific health issues, she insists you seek advice and support from your doctor or healthcare team first – especially if you have diabetes, as this needs to be assessed as being safe for you to try. Standing on the wobble cushion will test and exercise your balance, so always hold on to something to start with, and build up to standing without hanging on. Try to advance to one leg if you are able.

Footcare for hiking

Before you go

Hopefully, there will come a time when you want to move on to something more challenging than your daily outing with the dog, or a Sunday morning woodland walk with your partner, or a long day exploring the seashore.

At that point you are going to have to think about blisters, the enemy of the longer-distance walker. The first thing to know about blisters is that they have as much to do with the integrity of the skin on your feet as they do with your socks and shoes.

You have a lot of skin on your feet; under the sole, it can be up to 1cm thick, especially under the heel. It can also be very dry, building up where it shouldn't and then cracking into fissures.

Imagine what happens to the skin on your fingers when you wash up pots and pans by hand in hot water, or how prune-ish you look after a long soak in the bath. Your skin is so soft you could just peel it off in places. When your feet get hot and sweaty on a long walk, it's the same principle.

What you have to do is prepare them for this by slapping on a cream containing urea, which stops the body making changes to the composition of the skin. Keep them well creamed to reduce the danger of developing a blister. You can always change your socks halfway through a long walk – and I would advise you to do that – but prepping your feet is everything.

After you walk

Never rule out the benefits of a traditional footbath with Epsom salts. They're not expensive and can be very effective.

Massage your feet yourself, or better still, get someone else to do it for you! And run through the exercises on pages 188–9 to restore a full range of movement, rising up and down on your tiptoes, gripping with your toes, splaying them and wiggling them.

And finally . . . a note on high heels

Helen is one of Britain's leading authorities on high heels, so I had to ask for her thoughts.

She says: 'Historically, high heels were worn by rich and famous men to keep them away from the dirt on the streets. It's only been in the last sixty to seventy years they've become mainstream female fashion. And there are real biomechanical reasons why they look sexy.

'When you wear a heel more than four centimetres tall, it gets rid of the heel strike component of walking, and that means a longer stride. This extension makes you stick out your bottom and push your chest forward. It also changes your stride; instead of walking as though you were on train tracks, as we do normally, one foot goes in front of the other to give the pronounced wiggle you see in catwalk models. You have to walk that way in heels to achieve stability, because the additional height is translating all of your body weight forward.

'The downside is that you don't bend your knee as much as you do in flats, so your body puts more weight on your front foot. That's why your toes and the balls of your feet hurt even after you've taken your heels off – and, if you have bunions, that's why they ache, too. (That and the fact they're often squashed into the narrow pointy toe boxes we usually see on stilettos.)'

Speaking of bunions . . .

These days, bunions don't mean the end of beautiful shoes. There are a couple of leading shoe manufacturers specialising in footwear that accommodates bunions without compromising on style. Helen works with a company called Calla, which makes shoes and boots with extra wide toe boxes, invisible stretchy panels, strategically placed sandal straps and cushioned arches.

There's also Sole Bliss, whose six-inch snakeskin sandals have been spotted on the red-carpet feet of Julia Roberts, Rebel

Wilson and Viola Davies. Helen Mirren and Queen Camilla are also fans of the brand.

Last words from Helen

We take our feet for granted – and we shouldn't. Ensuring they are strong, healthy and functioning normally will help keep you walking – and healthier – for longer. Always ensure any podiatrist you consult is registered with the Health and Care Professions Council (hcpc-uk.org), and is qualified to assess gait.

8

Green Exercise: Walking and Working Out in Nature's Gym

'It's never too late to start over, never too late to be happy.'
Jane Fonda

When I left hospital, having been separated from my left breast, I promised myself I would get outside every single day of my life from then onwards. A cancer diagnosis does that to you. Every precious moment is amplified, and the chance to continue living comes with an aggressive edge of survivor mode.

That's how I felt, anyway.

Then, getting outdoors for a shuffle around the garden was my target. Today, I swipe myself in and out of nature's Green Gym for a decent workout every day. It is cheaper and closer than a conventional gym, it's always open, comes with free fresh air and sunlight, and smells better too.

To be outside is to feel and experience life in the round. When I'm sharing space with a tree, breathing in cold, cloudy air or staring at the fractal patterns of a pine cone, I feel happy, in awe of the magic of nature and content with my place in it.

I love looking up at the night sky and seeing stars that are actually in the past. Sirius, the brightest star in the sky (you might know it as the Dog Star), is about eight and a half light years away from Earth, which means when you look at it twinkling, you're seeing it as it was eight and half years ago. (You know I like to get my Greek references in and Sirius comes from the Greek word *Seirios*, which means glowing or scorching.)

If only we could turn our own clocks back like that: what would you do differently?

Me, I would have exercised routinely. I've always been active, I've always exercised, but not the way I do now. Recovering from cancer has taught me that to keep body systems working well, you need to carve out an hour at least four times a week. That might sound daunting, but one in six deaths in the UK is caused by inactivity.[1] Although you might feel as though doing a dozen push-ups will kill you, it won't.

Physical inactivity? That will. I don't want you to be put off by my goals, if all you can manage is ten minutes a few times a week then I encourage you to do that. The most important thing it to get started and build these new habits into your life.

We may be adults, but our bodies still need movement just as they did when we were babies. A study by New York University revealed the average toddler clocks up almost 2,400 steps an hour, and more than 14,000 steps a day.[2] These steps (including lots of falls) are important for their physical growth, and also increase their perception, memory and language.

These benefits do not stop as we age. If you're physically active, your heart is conditioned to beat slower and stronger, and it needs less oxygen to function well. Your arteries become springier, so they push your blood along more efficiently, and your levels of 'good' HDL cholesterol rise. Physical activity also helps prevent type 2 diabetes; when your muscles are used to working, they stay more receptive to insulin, the hormone that ushers blood sugar into the cells. If you're fit, blood sugar levels aren't as likely to creep up.

Moving the body helps the brain, too. Several studies have found that exercise can reduce symptoms of depression, changing the brain in ways similar to antidepressant medication. In older age, physical activity can delay the slide of cognitive decline into dementia and, even after the process has started, exercise, alongside exposure to light at the right time of day, can improve certain aspects of thinking.

I accept that exercising a minimum of four times a week is a big ask. Most of us are ridiculously busy from the moment we open our eyes until we close them again. Humans used to live in tribes that offered a supportive circle of help for our homes, families and work. Today in the Western world, most of us live in a 'progressive' nuclear family, which means every duty and commitment falls to an individual – that's you or me. There are no experienced grandparents to help with baby's night feeds, no kind cousin to cook a meal, no friendly neighbour who'll wait in for the plumber while we're at the office. Often, every detail of daily life is down to us, 24/7. We feel there isn't a second to spare. I know I do.

Adopting a healthier lifestyle with exercise built into it requires us to commit to change. It means we must implement different routines and make choices that aren't necessarily straightforward options. One of the best ways is to change your mindset on the days you are struggling. Think *What is my minimum for today* instead of *What is my maximum* (so think *I am going to do at least five reps* instead of *I need to do ten reps*) and you will be surprised what you accomplish in the end.

Also, here's the really great thing about nature's Green Gym – you can multi-task in it. You can walk and work out while soaking up the benefits of daylight and focusing on your breath – and, if you go with a friend or loved one, nurture your relationships along the way. Plus, as I said earlier, it's cost-free. Walking out of your own front door is one of the easiest and best things you can do for your physical and mental health.

Discovering green exercise

Movement and wellness coach Hannah Beadle lives and breathes outdoor exercise. Her company Wildfitness runs fitness retreats deep in nature across Europe – and in Iceland, too. At the end of this chapter you will find her specially created programme, designed to help you find your fitness in green spaces.

Hannah was once a competitive squash player, trained from the age of six to do traditional exercises repeatedly until she'd got them right. She was a fully qualified personal trainer by the age of eighteen and, in her own words, 'thought I wasn't doing my job well enough unless my client was on the floor, exhausted, by the end of their training session'.

In 2015, she stumbled across the concept of green exercise, and today her approach is radically different.

> As a species, we are meant to be outside, not confined to screens and chairs, stuck behind four walls. Green exercise, moving as humans should be moving, through nature, is within us all. It's intuitive, because you are connecting with an old part of yourself – you already know how to do it. Nobody ever says, 'I am going outside to make my biceps bigger.' They say, 'I'm upset so I am going for a stomp around the block to calm down.' Your body will tell you what it needs, if you remember how to listen.
>
> Green exercise offers adaptability, resilience, interaction and connection. Walking is at the heart of that.
>
> You might think 'it's just a walk', but it never is. Are you walking to build muscle or clear your head? What is your intention? Are you walking for fun with a friend? Is this the time for a therapeutic conversation with a loved one? Or do you simply need to be alone outside, widening your gaze?

Hannah knows few of us are able to regularly hike twenty kilometres as she does, but she says that when you make green exercise a way of life, even a few minutes counts, and you cannot quantify the benefits.

> If you are on uneven terrain, you are going to hop from point to point, incorporating a bunch of mini-jumps without even realising it. You might climb a steep slope with a 'bear' crawl

and 'crab' your way back down. Balance will come into play
when you cross a stream or climb a barrier. Who knows what
will happen if you encounter a fallen tree which is blocking
your path: will you go over, under or around it? And how?

When it's winter, you'll be working on your stability as you
move over ice. If it's a wet day, we all jump over puddles to try
to keep our feet dry. See how many different movements you
do unconsciously while 'just' walking?

This kind of green exercise is not a rural concept. Cambridge University's Department of Architecture has been looking at the positive impact on public health of adding obstacles such as balance beams and stepping stones into urban landscapes in order to improve our cardiovascular health, bone density and balance.[3]

I'm always jumping up on to little walls or balancing on kerb-stones when I walk my children to school, because – of course – they do it too, without thinking.

We'll be exploring how you can incorporate green exercise into your life later in the chapter, but first, I want to talk about why you should.

 Blue Zones

I love Greece, home of Aristotle's Peripatetic School, and part of my heritage. There's one particularly remote part of Greece that demands our attention in this chapter, though: the island of Ikaria in the far east of the Mediterranean.

Ikaria is one of the world's so-called Blue Zones, the five areas identified as places where humans live longest. They're fascinating and diverse: Okinawa in Japan, Sardinia in Italy, Nicoya in Costa Rica, Loma Linda in California, and Ikaria, where one in three people survive into their nineties. Islanders have lower rates of cancer and heart disease, suffer less depression and dementia, maintain a sex life into their eighties and enjoy active, healthy, happy lives, even as they head towards their century.[4]

Dan Buettner is an explorer and educator (and now *New York Times* best-selling author) who was part of the team that first identified these fascinating places. In his book *Blue Zones: 9 Lessons for Living Longer*, he suggests that only twenty-five per cent of our longevity is decided by our genes, while 'the other 75% is determined by our lifestyles and the everyday choices we make'. He's not talking about anything radical here, but about 'a constellation of little things that add up'.

He is very clear that one of these things is walking in nature.[5] It's no coincidence that three of the world's five longevity hotspots – Okinawa, Sardinia and Ikaria – are located in narrow, steep regions where inhabitants spend their days marching up and down hills. You might not live in one of them, but the life-enhancing blueprint of these Blue Zones is there for you to follow, wherever you are.

Nature for life

From being a little girl unwittingly soaking up vitamin N with my dad while walking across the Peak District, to the showbiz years of my twenties when I would walk home from friends' houses in Los Angeles (much to their amazement), I have always intrinsically known that being in green spaces, walking and connecting to the earth, is somehow good for us. Today, there's plenty of empirical evidence to back up that gut feeling, and it's clear that walking is already playing a significant role in the recovery of people with long Covid.

While I've been writing this book, I have also been filming in Ireland for Channel 4. In Dublin, I went to talk to neuroscientist Professor Shane O'Mara, professor of experimental brain research at Trinity College, Dublin. (I have mentioned him a couple of times already in this book.) He's a big walker, and has written a book called *In Praise of Walking*, which takes a scientific look at its benefits.

He told me: 'If you take people in their late sixties and early seventies . . . and get them to exercise regularly, taking a decent walk three times a week, the age-related performance of their memory comes back from, say, the early seventies to the late sixties, a gain in function of a year or two years.'

Shane and I also talked about something called BDNF: brain-derived neurotrophic factor. He explains this in simple terms as 'fertiliser for neurons', but it's only produced by neurons when they are active, not when they are inactive. And how do we get neurons to be active? Bingo! By moving, exercising and getting out and about; by challenging ourselves; by generally keeping our brains and bodies busy.

Reading this chapter and talking about it with your friends later will do the trick. Try doing it while you're out walking, preferably somewhere you can see the colour green – as I said, multi-task! And while you're at it, go as briskly as you can. A major study of 400,000 British adults by the University of Leicester shows that a faster walking pace is linked to a lower biological age. As little as ten minutes of brisk walking a day is associated with longer life expectancy – so get a shifty on![6]

The importance of seeing green

A study by the University of Essex suggests that exercising while looking at green – fields, trees, hedges, lawns, leaves, the algae on a canal – raises our energy levels and helps keep our mood on an even keel.[7] It's thought this bodily response stretches back to the time of early man, when lush greenery meant abundant food and water was close at hand.

The University of Essex project was far from comprehensive – it focused solely on men in their twenties, all of whom lived in the UK – but it is backed by the science of colour therapy, which tells us green is the colour of life, renewal and energy. It balances our emotions and leaves us feeling secure.

The Spanish playwright Pedro Calderon de la Barca, writing in Madrid back in the early 1600s, said: 'Green is the prime colour of the world and that from which its loveliness arises.'

I'm not sure anyone in the last four centuries has put it better.

Exercise and age: beyond walking

Some would argue that walking on its own is good enough as regular exercise, and if you're struggling to get into a routine, I would recommend it as your foundation, but there's another body system that mustn't be overlooked.

If you're over thirty and not doing any sort of load-bearing exercise, it's likely that you're suffering from age-related sarcopenia. (If it doesn't sound that serious to you, try it in Greek, where it literally translates to 'poverty of flesh'.) It begins between thirty and forty years of age, and it's the delightful process of losing muscle mass and function. Physically inactive people can lose as much as three to five per cent of their muscle mass each decade after thirty. Evidence suggests that skeletal muscle mass and skeletal muscle strength decline in a linear fashion, with up to fifty per cent of mass lost by the time you are eighty.

The good news is, it's simple to combine walking with strength training outside. What I mean here is strength training without dumb bells and kettle bells, but using your own bodyweight.

It's not about looking buff (something that has definitely become less important to me as I get older), because 'muscle' is about a lot more than aesthetics. Skeletal muscle plays a key role in postural retention (keeping us upright) and locomotion (letting you undertake the everyday physical activities of human life), but over the last twenty years, scientists have also come to regard the skeletal muscular system as an endocrine organ, meaning it secretes hormones and other products directly into the blood.[8]

Your muscles 'talk' to the brain and other systems around the body when you use them – or, to be more specific, when you contract them through weight-bearing exercise. This is thought to have positive effects on everything from cognitive function to blood sugar levels. There is growing epidemiological evidence that a physically active life plays an important role in helping protect humans against type 2 diabetes, cardiovascular diseases, cancer, dementia and even depression.

The science is new, it's complicated, but in a nutshell what we know is this: skeletal muscle is the largest organ in the human body, and working it is very good for you, as it seems to offer 'exercise-induced protection' against several chronic diseases. Professor Bente Klarlund Pedersen in Copenhagen is pushing back the boundaries of research here. Her team's work may eventually enable doctors to prescribe types and amounts of exercise for people who, like me, have had a cancer diagnosis, or those with diabetes or neurodegenerative diseases.[9]

 ## The significance of muscle

I spoke to New York-based functional medicine practitioner Dr Gabrielle Lyon, founder of the Institute for Muscle-Centric Medicine, who specialises in brain and thyroid health, lean body mass support and longevity. As well as having a global patient list, she also works with Special Operations soldiers to ensure their optimum health.

I asked her why we have 'missed' the importance of muscles in relation to overall health until relatively recently?

She tells me: 'We have missed the significance of muscles in the past because the focus was typically on "fat" and obesity. Society has focused on losing fat, whereas we now know that the emphasis should be on muscle (the organ of longevity).

Losing fat is beneficial, but building muscle helps us lose fat in the process, while improving many other health markers. While fat is a "symptom" of impaired muscle, improving and prioritising muscle can change the trajectory of ageing and protect our longevity.'

So WHY is this endocrine system so important?

'This endocrine system supports better blood sugar regulation and secretes myokines, which are proteins that help regulate metabolism in all other tissues of the body. The "muscle endo-crine system" helps improve androgen receptor expression in our reproductive system, decreases inflammation and improves our lipid profiles, boosts our immune system, improves mitochondrial function and insulin sensitivity.'

And what are your three top tips for building muscle mass healthily?

1. EAT MORE PROTEIN – at least 30 grams per meal (assuming you are having three meals a day) and never less than 100 grams of protein daily. When we shift our focus to protein-centred meals, all other macros easily fall into place.

2. Strength train – lift weights. This is the best way to build muscle mass and maintain it, along with a high protein diet.

3. Sleep – getting adequate sleep improves recovery, helps balance our circadian rhythm, and is where a large amount of muscle protein synthesis takes place. We need restful sleep as part of a routine to build and maintain muscle.

Finally, in simple terms, what are type I and type II muscle fibres (and, yes, we do need to know this!)?

'Type I fibres are slow-twitch fibres, which makes them relatively fatigue resistant. These produce more energy and are best for long, aerobic exercise. Type II fibres are fast oxidative glyco-lytic, which are less fatigue resistant and have higher or faster twitch speeds. They are best utilised for short, fast bursts of activity that do not require as much oxygen. While this information is not vital for someone looking to improve overall health and build muscle, using and working both type I and type II muscle fibres is important for overall well-being. Therefore, you would ideally want to incorporate a combination of Zone 2 cardio/ aerobic exercise, as well as HIIT into your workout regime.'

You can find out more about Gabrielle's work by going to https://drgabriellelyon.com. Her book *Forever Strong, A New Science-Based Strategy for Ageing Well* is due out late 2023.

Get started now

For this book, Hannah has devised a series of exercises designed to be done in a garden or a park, on the beach or in open countryside. Alongside walking, they form the core of human movement patterns. You'll find them at the end of this chapter, with illustrations to guide you.

Hannah says:

Choose what you need, see what the day calls out to you. And whatever you do, don't call it a workout! The vocabulary used around fitness can be negative. Why 'work out' when you have already done a day's work, or when you have a day's work ahead of you? It's not a chore. Say instead, 'Great, I can go for a walk!'

Any time you can devote to movement is beneficial. Doing five minutes is better than not doing five minutes. Balance at the bus stop, sit in a resting squat while you are boiling the kettle, hang from a tree branch when you find one that's a comfortable height for you.

Do a multiplicity of different movements in different places, and remember that as human beings, we are meant to experience different textures and different temperatures, too. Don't wrap yourself up in winter – when you put the bin out, go in your T-shirt and let yourself feel the cold. It's as different from our centrally heated life as the feel of a polished dining table is to the bark of a living tree.

Improved health and well-being are the result of how we live our lives in these small, natural ways. It is not about a gym membership and a training schedule. When you understand that, it's transformational.

Whether you have ten minutes to spare or a luxurious half morning set aside, get out and get going in nature's Green Gym, stretching your legs and flexing your muscles.

Julia's top tips for getting motivated

- It is always hard to start an exercise programme – and even harder to keep going. Finding emotional support is key. Who is the person who can meet you at 6am so you can run together, or who will encourage you out in the evening despite the fact you've had a long day?
- Apps can be really useful tools for this too, nudging you along.
- Don't let people who want to stay at home being inactive (movie, sofa, biscuit tin) stop you. Find someone, or something, to help motivate you instead.
- For me, it's simple – if I exercise, the chance of my breast cancer coming back decreases by approximately twenty per cent. My determination to live longer so I can see my children grow up beats every groggy start, every temptation to take the escalator rather than the stairs, and even my longing to eat chocolate mousse after *every* meal.
- Things to motivate you: perhaps you want to be able to play with your grandchildren or, if you are younger, fitness and strength goals may be more motivating. Find your tribe of colleagues and friends who you can go on this journey with. Even if you can't get

together in person you can use social media and messaging to encourage one another. Getting fit for a long distance walk, a mountain you want to conquer or a charity you want to raise money for are all good motivational goals.

Exercises to connect you to nature

Hannah says:

The movements and patterns in this chapter, whether completed separately or together, form a practice designed to keep you present. True presence is something seldom found in modern life, in particular in a gym environment, with many of us simply going through the motions to get the job done with little thought as to how or why.

Humans live in a world full of rules, laws and instructions, constantly driving us to do the 'right' thing. You will learn the same lesson from nature that I did – it is OK to slow down. Movement and life are part of the same whole. We need to recognise and acknowledge what is happening within our lives (family stress, work deadlines) and act accordingly when choosing the movement practice appropriate for that specific day or period in our life.

That's not a free pass to do nothing or less than your best – it's about trusting yourself.

We have lost the connection to ourselves and the world around us. In order to reignite this spark, we want to encourage you to head outside. To feel the world around you, to interact with your environment and to move in the ways that nature intended.

Taking this path allows you to figure things out for yourself, to develop your own understanding and your own answers to the questions being asked. Your questions will be different every time you come to this practice and that is part of the joy of being out in nature.

Some points to note

Reps and sets: If you have ever been a member of a gym, attended a gym class or completed an exercise programme, then you will be used to seeing reps and sets next to each prescribed exercise. The movements in this chapter do not have reps and sets next to them. Why? Because we want you to embrace the ways of nature. Let go of the rules and rigidity of modern life. This prospect can be a little daunting at first, but stick with it. Go with the flow and listen to what your body needs at that moment in time. Take the opportunity to explore and experiment with each movement, to add your own personality and flair when the moment grabs you.

You don't have to do everything in order: In fact, you do not even have to do everything in one go (that would be quite the training session)! We recommend that you pick and choose what your body is calling for that day. And if you only have a couple of minutes while your walking buddy pops into the coffee shop for that well-earned refreshment, then seize the chance to wiggle your spine in any way possible, hang from the scaffolding outside the shop next door, or simply breathe.

Alternatives: When you see the heading 'alternatives', that is us providing you with an alternative point of view on the task at hand. If you do not have a bench nearby, for example, then take a look at the alternatives.

Not everywhere is the same: The beauty of the natural world (and the urban one, for that matter), is that no one place is the same as anywhere else. Even your local park changes with the seasons. We want to encourage you to explore these movements in as many different environments and weathers as possible.

Look out for the star: When reading through the exercises, you will see a couple of movements with a star (*) next to them. These are the ones (due to their huge benefits) we recommend you try to do as often as possible throughout the week.

Warm-up exercises

Guideline: 30 seconds–1 minute per exercise
Warming up is an opportunity for you to check in with yourself, to think about your intentions for what is to come, and to extend a hand to nature and invite it to accompany you.

Neck mobility*

- In a kneeling position, slowly and consciously move your head from side to side, forward and back and in circles, breathing as you go.

Standing open-ups*

- Find a neutral stance. Begin by rounding your spine as much as possible and tilting your pelvis as if it was a bucket and you wanted to pour some water out the back.
- At the same time, straighten your arms out in front of you and bring the backs of the hands to meet, thumbs down, head tucked in.
- From here reverse the movement by bringing the arms outstretched to the sides, thumbs up and back. Open and extend the spine. Now tilt your pelvis as though you were pouring the water out of the front of that bucket and look up.
- Slowly move between the two positions, finding your breathing as you go.

Alternative: You can also complete this kneeling or sitting.
Note: Think standing cat-cow.

Paint the wall

- Find a tree, wall, climbing frame, hedge or any object with a surface area the size of half your armspan (roughly).
- Stand sideways on to your object, approximately a foot away from it. Stay in this spot throughout.
- From here, imagine the front and back of your hand is a paint-brush and you are trying to cover as much of your chosen object as possible with paint. Switch between your hands every thirty seconds or every minute if you can.

Note: For the first thirty seconds, keep the legs straight, feet still and spine as neutral as possible, forcing the movement to come from the shoulder, wrist and elbow. For the second thirty seconds, incorporate the whole body. Bend the knees, twist, pivot . . . give yourself more freedom and see where the arm takes you. Keep your feet in the same spot throughout.

T-twists

- Use the same object you used for the movement above. Stand approximately a foot away from it, facing it. (If comfortable, you can complete this in free space without anything in front of you.)
- Stand with your feet approximately shoulder-width apart, with a soft bend in the knees.
- From here (staying on the spot, feet facing forward at all times), raise both arms out to your sides.
- By rotating your torso, take your left arm out towards the right by threading it through the gap between yourself and your surface.
- Before returning, ensure that you extend your left arm as far as possible, while bringing your right behind the small of your back.

Note: As Joseph Pilates once said, 'You are only as young as your spine is flexible.' Remember, it is necessary to bend, twist, fold, extend and move your spine in any way possible (that does not cause pain, of course).

Wrist mobility

- Kneeling on the ground, place your hands flat on the ground in front of you, palms down, arms straight, elbows extended, fingers splayed and facing forwards. Slowly sway your weight from side to side and in circles around the wrist.
- Repeat this with the fingers of both hands facing out to the sides, and then facing towards you.
- Place the back of the hands on the floor, fingers facing in towards each other, and slowly try to straighten the elbows.

Note: If any of the ground movements are too much for your wrists during this practice, take a break, place the palms of your hands together and raise towards your sternum, fingers pointing to the floor (like a reverse prayer). You can also take hold of one wrist just below the wrist bone and gently pull to create a little traction and release pressure.

Restless foot – lower body mobility

- Get into an all-fours position (knees down for now), with your hands on the ground in front of you.
- Keep your left foot in contact with the floor, and start to explore with your right.
- Move, twist, turn, pivot, explore, and see what you come up with . . . swap feet and lift the knees whenever you want. (Try to cover as much of the floor as possible with the foot.)

Note: Do not overthink it! There is no right or wrong. Your body knows what it needs – let it tell you.

Gather

- Standing with a soft bend in the knees, ground yourself comfortably.
- Once you feel centred, breathe in and bring your arms from your sides and into a gentle prayer position above your head.

- When your hands are overhead, start your exhale and bring them down on either side into a gentle cup below the waist.
- Repeat two or three times.

Note: Try to breathe in and out through your nose.

Shake

- Stand upright. It can help to close your eyes for this one.
- Start bouncing/shaking on the spot, keeping at least the balls of your feet in contact with the ground throughout.
- Let your body do what it needs to. Let go of tension and let go of the breath. I shake my hands out and then let them swing freely around my body – it's a real release.
- After roughly a minute, let your arms hang by your sides and just take some time to breathe.

Main exercises

Balance practice*

As the saying goes 'life is all about balance'; it is at the root and core of everything we do. Like everything else, balance is a skill, and a fundamental one at that. Balance is one of the main keys to living a healthy and able life, to keep that connection between mind and body. It is, however, a skill that we often forget to include in our conscious practice.

A simple balance practice like this not only helps you to connect with yourself, but also encourages you to slow down physically and mentally. Take the opportunity to press pause on your day and watch life go by around you. Kick off your shoes to really connect to your environment, man-made or not.

- Find a low kerb, fallen log, edge of a flower bed, a simple plank of wood, or anything that you can balance on.

- Start by walking back and forth, turning at each end on the object instead of getting off and going back to the start.
- When comfortable, progress to standing on one leg at a time to see how long you can balance for. Move your free leg around and see what difference this makes to your centre of gravity.
- When walking along, stop and bend down to touch the object that you are balancing on before carrying on.
- If you are feeling particularly comfortable, start to take little hops from one foot to the other.

Alternative: If you cannot find anything to balance on, simply stand on one leg. Once you're used to this, move your free leg around to test your balance even more. Still stable? Close your eyes.

Note: Keep your head up and focus ahead. Your head is your heaviest point; if this drops, you will too.

Passive hang*

Hanging is one of the most beneficial movements you can include in your daily life (or as often as possible). Not only does it reverse the effects of gravity compressing your spine, but it also helps with grip strength, shoulder mobility and all-round shoulder health, wrist health and decompression. Hanging also promotes good posture and can aid proper breathing mechanics.

The life of the modern human is far removed from the way our ancestors used to swing and move through the trees. Because of this, the structure of our shoulders and their mechanics have changed over time, and we, as modern humans, have lost a lot of overhead range. Think how good it will feel if we can regain some of this.

Also, we live in a world of man-made materials that are smooth, finished and clean. Hanging outside allows us to feel the world around us and invites back into our lives different textures, surfaces, temperatures, and perhaps a little bit of dirt. Don't worry, though, you can always wash your hands afterwards.

- Find something stable and sturdy from which you are able to hang, such as a tree branch, scaffolding, climbing frame or swing set.
- Reach your hands overhead and relax, allowing your head to sink down into your shoulders (as if you're wearing your biceps as earmuffs).
- From here, if you are comfortable enough to ease some weight out of your feet or hang completely, then do so.
- If you're able to do so, then try adding a few pull-ups to the end of your hanging time.

Alternative: If you cannot find something to safely hang from, then simply find something to reach up towards (a doorframe, for example). Reach your arms overhead to the object and take a step forwards keeping your arms on the object overhead throughout. Try not to arch your lower back.

Note: Remember to breathe and relax into the hang. Trust your hands.

You can buy affordable pull-up bars. I have one in my son's bedroom, fixed across his doorway, and the whole family have regular hanging competitions. Whenever I pass it, I have a little swing. There is one of those annoying little longevity tests you can find online, and, supposedly, middle-aged men and women are meant to be able to hang for one minute with their feet off the ground. I have just managed it – with those horrible gym gloves on – but it's been a challenge. How about you?

Foot-hand crawl

This is great for learning core strength and stability. It also helps promote wrist health and is a great introduction to weight-bearing through the hands, something we don't often do as adults. A foot-hand hold can also help you improve your squat position. Take a picture of yourself and rotate it ninety degrees, and you will see what we mean.

We are incredibly complex creatures, capable of a wide array of movements. Crawling (or low-gate locomotion) is one of the first actions that we master as babies, but we quickly move on from it as soon as we learn to walk. Our bodies have not forgotten, however. They crave crawling patterns like this, which are innate within all of us.

- Start in an all-fours position with your wrists under your shoulders, knees under hips and toes tucked under. Hover your knees just a couple of centimetres off the floor, keeping a nice straight back.
- Hold this position and breathe (rest when needed).

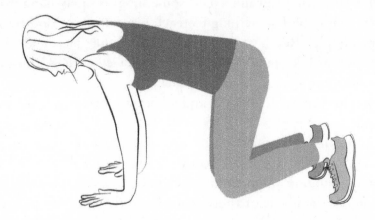

- When you're comfortable, start by lifting one hand and the opposite foot.

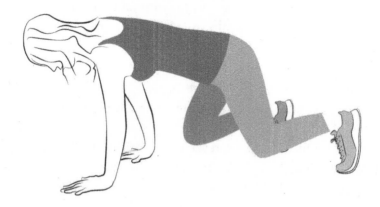

- Once you're happy with this, start to move forwards in small increments, keeping the hips low and still (balance a shoe on the small of your back to help this).
- Don't just go forwards and backwards. Try moving side to side, or diagonally . . . explore your space in as many ways as you can.

Note: Remember, this movement should be contralateral, meaning you're moving the opposite hand and foot. Try to be as soft as possible with the movement through both the feet and the hands.

Side-sit get-up

As we age, the majority of injuries don't come from falling but the inability to get up off the floor when we do fall. Start practising this skill now before it is too late.

Before the invention of chairs, we sat on the ground for everything that we did. As soon as we started sitting at ninety degrees, we lost the endless benefits that came with different ground-sitting positions. Now is your chance to regain what's been lost.

- Begin in a ninety-ninety or shin box position (see image 1 overleaf). This involves sitting with both knees and ankles at ninety degrees, with the torso as upright as possible.

- From this ninety-ninety position, your feet are going to remain stuck on the ground while your knees windscreen-wiper over to the other side.
- From here, raise yourself up on to your knees.
- Sweep your back leg to the front so that you are in a mini-lunge.
- From your lunge, stand up fully, or (if you have the mobility) open/lift up your back knee to bring yourself into a squat before standing. Once standing, reverse and repeat on the other side.
- Use your hands to help initially if needed. Alternatively, if progression is needed, then an external load can be added.

Note: Try to make this whole movement as smooth as possible. When you are comfortable and looking for a more advanced version, start to flow and play around with it to see what variations you can find. Perhaps add a small jump when you reach standing.

Pulling power

Bodyweight row

You never know when you will need to pull yourself up or over something. Practising a bodyweight row with different objects and at odd angles teaches your body to adapt and respond accordingly. It's also important to do a pull exercise like this one to balance the 'push' exercises that feature in this practice.

Find a horizontal object, such as safety rail or barrier, a tree branch, an outdoor table or any stable horizontal surface with nothing underneath that will get in your way. Try for around waist height – the lower it is, the harder the exercise. Lie face up underneath the bar/fence/branch and take hold of it with an underhand or overhand grip.

From here, keeping your body straight from head to toe, squeeze your glutes, keep your core tight and your chin tucked in, and pull your chest up to the rail. Pause at the top and return slowly, with control, until your arms are straight, repeat. As a progression, you can try this with one arm!

Lunge clock

Moving around the points of the clock allows you to access a fuller range of motion in the hips and ankles compared to traditional straight lunges. For example, when you take your right leg to nine o'clock, you will have to go into more of a curtsey. Very few things in nature are completely linear; our movements should reflect this.

- Imagine you are standing in the centre of a clock, facing twelve o'clock.

- With one leg, take a step back towards one point of the clock (this can be a large step or a small one, with your leg straight or bent). Come back to the centre and repeat, choosing different 'times' for each lunge.

Note: Some of these movements may look more like straight lunges or side lunges, while others look like slightly off-stance squats. There is no right or wrong here. As with all movements, we want you to explore.

Spinal rock to press

The various pressing positions in this movement challenge and stress the body in different angles and ranges compared to traditional press-ups. These presses give you the rare opportunity to get those hands on the ground, and experience different temperatures, textures and surfaces. But most of all, they allow you to take your heart that little bit closer to the earth.

- Start sitting on the ground, with your feet flat on the floor, and your chest hugged into your knees.
- From here, round your spine and gently roll back, with momentum, one vertebra at a time, until your hips lift off the ground. This is the peak of your roll.
- Once here, rock up again.
- When you reach the top of the rock, cross one leg underneath you and come up into a half kneeling position (as if you are about to propose).

- At this point, imagine you have a clock face around you. Take your hands out towards any point on the clock between nine and three o'clock and perform a press.
- Roll back and repeat on different points.

Note: Play around with how far out you take your hands. To make it easier at first, practise the spinal rocks to half kneeling, then practise the press separately, before connecting together. And remember, the ground is your teacher here. If it feels uncomfortable and 'clunky' on the spinal rocks, listen and take note. Round your spine a little more and control the movement . . . be gentle!

Jumps

Jumping is one of those endlessly beneficial movements for human beings, offering us everything from strength-building to improved bone density and coordination. Playing around with different variations and targets/terrain encourages creativity.

Have you heard the saying, 'If you change the way you look at things, the things you look at change'? The world is your playground. Look at your environment with a child's mind, and you will suddenly see, everywhere you go, endless things you can jump on, off, to and from.

- Find something you can use as a landing target: a crack in the pavement, a leaf, the kerb or a fallen log, for example.
- Start by squarely facing your chosen object. Take a two-footed jump on to it. Your aim here is to stick the landing for three seconds.
- Once you have achieved a few of these, your challenge is to see how many different jumps you can come up with and stick. For example, you may try jumping from two feet and landing on one, jumping from one foot and landing on one, or starting your jump from slightly further away from your object.

- For anything on the ground (like leaves and cracks), try sideways jumps too.

Note: Start small and progress. Land with soft knees, driven out. Your arms should be out in front of you as you land to act as a counterbalance, and you should aim to land on the ball of your foot with your heel slightly raised. The landing should be as quiet and soft as possible.

Lifting in nature

For the following exercise, you will need some kind of external weight. Try to go natural if you can, using things like rocks or logs. If this is not possible, then you can use sandbags, medicine balls, kettlebells, tyres or even a rucksack full of books.

Lifting in the natural world compared to lifting in a gym environment is about realism. In life, the things you need to lift don't often present themselves on a bar or attached to a machine. The ground you stand on isn't necessarily matted or perfectly flat, and unless you are lifting for aesthetic reasons, you are likely to be wanting to move the object somewhere. Real-world lifting can be humbling and teaches you all about adaptability, resilience, interaction and connection.

Deadlift and carry

From a physical point of view, deadlifts are great for developing strength in multiple areas, promoting stability and mobility, improving grip strength and encouraging foot activation.

- Choose your object; this could be a log, a rock or anything that you can find with a little weight behind it.
- Stand as close to your chosen object as possible, with your feet shoulder-width apart.
- Pretend you have some paper under your feet that you are trying to tear (in other words, screw your feet into the ground).
- From here, bend and get a good grip on the chosen object. Once your grip is established, lift your hips slightly above knee height, imagining a wooden pole running down your back, touching the back of your head, the top of your back (between your shoulder blades) and the small of your back.

- Take a deep breath into the belly.
- Keeping a straight back, drive away from the floor to stand up, exhaling when the weight reaches your knees. Once upright (if possible), take the weight for a walk (this part is very important), and drop it when you are done, watching out for your toes.

Note: Real-world lifting does not always allow you to have faultless technique. The tips above are the foundation of a 'correct' lift to use where possible. Remember, you are only weak in the movements, positions and patterns that you don't practise. Challenge yourself with different objects, weights and shapes when practising your deadlifts.

Wind-down exercise

This is an opportunity to simply *be*. To move without instruction and thought. An opportunity to bring out a bit of that inner child, to interact with nature in one of the purest ways possible and reconnect to your roots.

Tree flow

- Find a tree (oaks are brilliant) or a climbing frame/structure in your garden or local park. Unleash your inner child and simply climb.
- Once you are comfortable, start to interact with the object, trying to create a flow or a sequence as you move.
- A starting point is to think *over, under, around*. Keep repeating this pattern and see what you come up with.

Note: Tune in to the sounds of nature to help you connect with your movement. Let go of any inhibitions and just try to make your movements as smooth and fluid as possible. If you have any little ones in your life, observe how they move and try to copy.

Alternative: If you cannot find a suitable tree or climbing frame, instead locate a bench or railing. How many ways can you go on to, over, under and – in the case of some benches – through it?

Cool-down exercises

Guideline: At least 1 minute per exercise
Your cool-down is your opportunity to slow down. To appreciate, thank and send some love back to your body for all it has accomplished today.

Seated mobility

- Sit on the ground. You could be crossed-legged, kneeling, with your legs straight, or a mixture of these.
- From here, simply move! Bend, twist, reach . . . listen to your body. Remember, this is a cool-down so take it slowly and do not rush. Aim for at least five minutes if you can.

Note: If there are any particular areas of your body that feel tighter than others, pay attention! Don't ignore them . . . they feel tight for a reason, and these are the areas that need the most work.

Lying mobility

- Lie down in a supine position (on your back) and move. Hug your knees, circle your ankles, gently roll from side to side, reach out, hold a 'happy baby' yoga pose. Move in any way you feel you need to.

Breathe*

- Once you have completed your mobility, straighten your legs or sit up in a crossed-leg position and simply breathe.

- You can start by placing one hand on your chest and the other on your stomach (remember, we want the lower hand to be moving here, not the upper).
- Try one of the relaxing breathing exercises from Chapter 5 here, and remember to try to breathe lightly in and out of your nose.
- Remain here for as long as you need.

Grounding

Barefoot in the grass

You might not be old enough to remember the scene in *Pretty Woman* where Vivian (Julia Roberts), a smiley part-time prostitute ('the tart with a heart'), gets stroppy billionaire businessman Edward (played by Richard Gere) to take his shoes and socks off to walk on the grass in a park – and it makes him feel good. With reason. Grounding is as old as the hills. Literally. Walking barefoot is a deeply calming restorative thing to do. Your body swaps electrons with the earth and the benefits are said to include better sleep, a change in blood viscosity, the lowering of inflammation and improved mood. Think about how good you feel when you've been barefoot on the beach all day. That's partly because of being outside all day, swimming in the sea, and grounding. I am *not* going to site a study here (although there are many), I'm going to encourage you to try it yourself because, besides from stepping in some bird poo, there are no risks. And you can get grounding shoes and flip flops if you are worried about the poo.

Remember, in the words of Kermit, the most famous frog in the world: 'It's not easy being green,' so good luck and give it your best.

9

Walks of Your Lifetime

'If you think adventure is dangerous, try routine, it's lethal.'
Paul Coelho, in a tweet from 2011

This is not a how-to or where-to chapter – you've got the internet for that. (Though if it was me, I'd be in the travel section of my local bookshop, a destination in its own right. You know the sort of place, where the only flight you need is a flight of fancy.)

I want this chapter to be a *why*-to: *why* you should think about doing an epic, life-enhancing walk, the walk of your lifetime.

I've already done one from the 'World Walks' list – Iceland. I'd label it a walk of my lifetime for the scenery alone, but also for the updraft, which lifted me when I was struggling with infertility and didn't know how to lift myself. Sitting here, writing this, as a mother of three children, fulfilled and happy, I am eternally grateful for it.

But now cancer has bisected my life. I am not the person I was before my diagnosis. She was blissfully ignorant (and that didn't make her lesser, just different) about how it feels to confront your own mortality.

You don't need a chronic illness to face up to your ephemeralness. A landmark birthday – or, more profoundly, the death of a parent or a loved one – can make us question our temporary state. We joke about it, borrowing the language of death to amplify a feeling. How often have we 'almost died' of laughing, or of embarrassment, or threatened to 'kill' someone who's left their laundry on the floor? Sometimes, life gives us something so glorious – a meal, a view, a personal or professional triumph – that we announce we could 'die happy now'.

When you have cancer and you understand you might die for real, much sooner than expected, it's terrifying, and it would be weird if it didn't change you.

So I think now I have another walk of my lifetime to come, one of healing and gratitude and absolute joy that I was given another chance.

Here, I'm listing five epic and inspiring world walks to get you imagining what you might like to do. As I said at the very start of this book, walking is never about just putting one foot in front of the other. Walks can be a spiritual journey, or the hunt for something unique in nature, or, as that opening quote from Paul Coelho suggests, they can be about escaping the dangers of the everyday. (Coelho's enduringly popular 1980s novel *The Alchemist* is about a shepherd boy who walks from Andalucia to Egypt in search of treasure, only to find that what he's looking for is within him, not buried in the desert. It's a book about the power of dreams and the importance of listening to your heart. I have never been a fan of magical realism – I'm more likely to lose myself in one of Alfred Wainwright's guides to the Lakes or some of Malcolm Gladwell's realism – but I love the message of *The Alchemist*.)

It will take a bit of magical thinking to find the time and the funds to do one of these world walks, so the second part of this section is devoted to treks closer to home that can be tackled with a Bank Holiday weekend, a train ticket and a couple of nights in an Airbnb.

Five world walks

Japan's blossom season and the impermanence of life

I wouldn't go so far as to say I'm a Buddhist, but it's definitely the only religion I feel any affinity towards. There is a Japanese word originating in Buddhism that means impermanence and transience: *mujō*. All things are impermanent and continually subject to change, especially nature. I've always wanted to do the Nakasendō walking trail in Japan, to take in the flowering blossoms during that short window in spring when petals riot across the country. *Hanami* is the ancient Japanese custom of enjoying the transient beauty of flowers, and it almost always refers to the cherry blossoms. I can't think of a better reason to get a crick in your neck on a hiking holiday! Nakasendō was the mountain route that connected Kyoto to Tokyo in Japan's feudal era. It was walked by Samurai, merchants, the rich and the poor, all of whom, no matter their status, stopped footsore and hungry at the same sixty-nine resting points along the way. One of them is the mountain village of Yoshino, where 30,000 cherry trees (more than two hundred different varieties) carpet the area, blazing for just a fortnight before the blossom falls and dies.

The message from Japan's blossom-covered mountains: *Pay attention to all your days.*

Nature at its most natural in America's Yellowstone National Park

Yellowstone National Park will be a familiar name to you: a vast reserve stretching from the north-west corner of Wyoming into Montana and Idaho. (If that doesn't ring any bells, you may not have heard of the epic TV series starring Kevin Costner – but I digress.) In real life, the natural drama of Yellowstone has been unfolding for centuries. Most recently in 1995, the grey wolf was reintroduced and had a significant impact: beavers and elks have flourished, the water quality of the rivers has improved, and vegetation including young willow, aspen and cottonwood plants has thrived. But why – and how – have the wolves influenced all this? Well, it's a complex web but one example is that since the reintroduction of wolves, the elks have had to keep moving because of predatory pressure. Before this, they didn't move around as much in the winter, grazing heavily on young willow trees. Now that the elks have got a wiggle on, the willows have been free to flourish along the streams, and this has helped the beavers, who need willows to survive in winter. The beavers, in turn, are having a positive impact on the rivers and fish populations. It truly is the wonder of nature. In Yellowstone, you can see geysers and hot springs, grizzly bears and cougars, huge canyons and lakes – though sadly, you probably won't see a wolf, because in the wild they are secretive and shy.

The message from Yellowstone: *Nature always outdoes human 'progression' – and sometimes the way things were, is the way things should be.*

Finding a sense of perspective amid Iceland's fire and ice

Iceland is otherworldly; there's no other way to describe one of the most geologically dynamic countries on the planet, where thirty-two active volcanic systems erupt every four years on average. It sits across two tectonic plates (the Eurasian and North American), and even though there are plenty of other places where two continental plates drift apart, most of them are deep underwater. The section of the Mid-Atlantic Ridge on show above sea level here is part of the longest chain of mountains on the globe, at around 65,000 kilometres. Since ninety per cent of those mountains are beneath sea level, this is the only place you won't have to swap your walking boots for a snorkel, and it offers a smorgasbord (or a *hlaðborð*, as they call it in Iceland) of drop-dead amazing scenery. Some geologists think Iceland formed about sixty million years ago, and whatever the exact timing, the process hasn't stopped. Magma continues to find its way to the surface, and this lava is how Icelandic volcanoes are created and kept active. You can see around thirty of them in the south of the island, or take a hiking trail around one closer to Reykjavík. A long-distance challenge like the Laugavegur trail leads you through black volcanic rock, spouting thermal vents, lakes, gorges, glaciers and multicoloured rhyolite mountains. This constant movement means you can visit one year and, by the following year in the exact same spot, the landscape could have sprouted another mountain.

The message from Iceland: *To be here is a constant reminder that life moves on, with or without you, and that change is inevitable.*

Following in the footsteps of pilgrims to Santiago de Compostela in Spain

The Camino de Santiago is one of the great time-worn pilgrim trails of the world. It is not just one route, but a network of nine major paths, each with its own unique history and sights. The most famous is probably the 800-kilometre Camino Frances, which features in many books, movies and documentaries. Whichever way you take, all roads lead to the Catedral de Santiago de Compostela, believed to be the final resting place of St James. On the way, the Camino Frances passes through amazing cities such as Pamplona, and important pilgrim towns like Saint-Jean-Pied-de-Port, Logroño, Ponferrada and Sarria, via mountains and picturesque villages. Shell markers in bright yellow point the way for the thousands who walk it every year – and if one of them is you, then be prepared for serious hiking, because the average daily walking distance is twenty to twenty-five kilometres. For some people, this remains a religious route, but mostly the pilgrims have been replaced by hikers on a bonding experience with family and friends, escaping everyday life or seeking personal fulfilment and enrichment. Whether you are religious or not, it's important to remember that in the Middle

Ages, as many as 200,000 worshippers a year trod these steps. A whole infrastructure was built for them, including hospitals and places to stay, and orders of knights to protect them. Kings and ambassadors had to agree their safe passage. An inscription on the path reads: 'Europe was made on the Camino to Santiago', so this history of help and hospitality is significant and unifying.

The message from Santiago de Compostela: *You're not the first person to be here, nor will you be the last.*

How not to get eaten by a lion on foot in South Africa's Kruger Park

If I ask you to consider landscapes and experiences in South Africa, you'll probably think of Cape Town and the magnificent Table Mountain, visiting southern right whales on the Western Cape near Hermanus, or a safari to see the Big Five: rhinos, lions, buffalos, leopards and elephants. All very special. But how about a hike through the famous Kruger National Park? Yes, that's right, on foot. This is one of South Africa's largest game reserves, with a high density of animals, including the Big Five and hundreds of smaller mammals, together with a huge range of birds from vultures and eagles to storks and starlings. Think about that for a moment: seeing these creatures and experiencing the forests and bush plains, *not* from a four-by-four, but as a biped. You feel it, smell it and sense it at ground level, becoming a part of the wildlife, rather than an observer. There are only seven of these wilderness trails in the park, and numbers are restricted to minimise human impact. May to October is the best time for game viewing and walking safari conditions, because the vegetation is low and sparse, making animals easier to spot and track. When I trekked across the Kruger we saw monkeys, impala, kudu buffalo, elephants and giraffes. We also saw leopard tracks, and had an extremely cortisol-heightening encounter with a large (and territorial) male white rhino. Jaco, my guide, suddenly stopped in his tracks in front of me and the crew, and pressed an index finger to his lips. He made urgent movements, indicating we should stop walking and shut up. He told us to move behind what looked like a tiny twig to me – part of a fallen tree. I've never been so close to a rhino. It was a heart-stopping moment, and there's no way it would have been half as exciting looking on from a truck. The rhino started snorting and clearly didn't like us being in his space. Jaco knew what to do and how to behave, bravely moving away from us and making noises to distract the giant creature. There's a reason why the collective noun is a 'crash' of rhinoceroses. We carefully reversed out of the area, moving well clear and changing direction.

They say you feel the soul of a country when you walk through it; there is certainly nothing like hiking through the African bush, encircled by the crazy-beautiful sounds and aromas, knowing that you could stumble upon an extraordinary creature at any moment. If you want to feel alive and truly bound to earth, there is little to rival this.

The message from the Kruger: *There isn't any Wi-Fi in the bush, but I promise you will find no better connection.*

Five British walks

The UK is a serious walking destination with a mouthwatering diversity of environments. We are a small island, yet we have mountains and moors, crashing seas, luscious *Wind in the Willows*-style riverbanks, great fields of golden barley and tangly hedgerows filled with a symphony of birdsong.

These walks are ones I have done and loved myself, and in my notes on them, I'll tell you why.

One is part of Bradbury family folklore; another is the walk that helped me navigate my way to nature and walking for work. They stretch from *Poldark* and clotted-cream country in Cornwall, almost 800 miles north to the Inner Hebrides. The last one takes you from our west coast to our east, so you can dip your boot in the Irish Sea, facing the Atlantic and America, and then dunk it in the North Sea, gazing across to Europe and the Netherlands.

I can't think of a better metaphor for a great walk – something that connects you with both yourself and the rest of the world.

A helping hand

Ever since my first TV walks were broadcast – *Wainwright's Walks* way back in 2007 – I have been inundated with emails and letters and, in the last ten years, messages on social media asking me for advice about walking routes, walking boots and a variety of related topics ranging from maps to snacks.

This is how my sister Gina and I came to create The Outdoor Guide website www.theoutdoorguide.co.uk. It's a free online resource to encourage and support people who want to enjoy the great outdoors. It features hundreds of free walks that can be downloaded or perused for inspiration, and information about landmarks, food and drink stops, places you can stay, the gear you'll need and accessibility.

More recently Gina and I launched The Outdoor Guide Foundation to enable disadvantaged children across the UK to get outside. Children these days spend far less time outside than they did and, frighteningly, there are some youngsters who rarely get out at all – and we know how valuable fresh air and sunshine is to all of us.

The scheme is called 'Waterproofs and Wellies' and, as the name suggests, companies, organisations and individuals can get involved to provide waterproofs and wellies to state-school children who need them. It gives them the basic kit they need to have fun outside – not having such kit is one of the two main barriers to outdoor play. (The other is – sadly – not having family members willing and able to accompany and encourage them.)

If you can help please visit https://theoutdoorguidefounda-tion.org/

My heartsong: Dovedale Walk in the Peak District

In my family, we call the Dovedale Walk in the Peak District the Lovedale Walk. My dad was born nearby, and we started walking here together when I was tiny. This particular route is a family classic, an incredibly bonding, multi-generational walk. The Dove is a beautiful river with fast sections, long glides, tumbling weirs and deep pools. You can take a detour from it to climb Thorpe Cloud, a jagged 287-metre peak, from where you get a sweeping view across the dales and the meandering waters below. Then there's a pretty gorge, where the famous Dovedale Stepping Stones await. They were put there in Victorian times to encourage tourism – although in today's Instagram era, you're lucky if you don't have to queue for half an hour to hop across. (I think I must have been about seven when my walking boots first made contact. No Instagram.)

The Dove is a famous fishing river – trout, barbel, grayling and chub – and Dad taught me to tickle trout in a small stream nearby when I was about ten (this forbidden activity is utterly frowned upon now). I interviewed him about it on one of my TV walks, and he said that 'tickling your first trout is a bit like your first woman; slippery at first touch and completely unforgettable'. That soundbite remained in the final edit. I still have the scars. Thanks, Dad.

Trout tickling has become part of Bradbury family folklore. Dad taught his eldest grandson Jack (who's now twenty-five), my sister Gina's son, and, on a recent family trip to the Peak District, when we all climbed Mam Tor, we waded my three children in their wellies and waterproofs into another little stream, to give them a taster. We encouraged them to feel under the ledges of the riverbank to see if 'they could find any fish'. We knew they wouldn't, it was too cold – I mean, it was freezing – but watching them splashing around in a Peak District stream with my dad made my heart overflow with happiness. They'll never do what I did when I was a girl but I know that similar stories and the experience are stored somewhere in their heads.

There's no other landscape that says family and continuity to me as loudly as this one. When I was at my weakest, I knew that the Peaks would help me heal.

The message from the Peak District: *Whenever you face an emotional mountain, climb it with courage, faith and love.*

The mountain that made my career compass point in a different direction: Helvellyn in the Lake District

Walkers have been climbing hills for fun since the latter half of the eighteenth century, when hiking became popular. Helvellyn, with multiple routes up to its 950-metre peak, has always been among the nation's favourites, and came first in a popularity poll run in conjunction with my 2018 series *Britain's Top 100 Walks*. For me, it has a deep personal resonance, too – I owe my current career to the Lake District and, in part, to this mountain. I was presenting the consumer show *Watchdog* on BBC One with Nicky Campbell and getting six million viewers a week, when I found myself having a cup of tea with a commissioner for the much less mighty BBC Four. I liked the programmes on the channel; they were quirky, and I knew that as a broadcaster, I had to keep learning, expanding. The commissioner was considering a series about the walks of Alfred Wainwright, which, in all likelihood, would be presented by some beardy bloke, once he found one. I told him about my dad and our walking, and then there I was, in my cagoule, getting the job and going in a completely different career direction. I loved the fact that I could be in my power-suit taking corporate offenders to task onscreen on a Wednesday for *Watchdog*, and then striding up the likes of Helvellyn, introducing an entirely different audience to the Lakes on a Monday. *Wainwright Walks* first aired in 2007, and it was to be the map for the next fifteen years of my career. Whenever I get the chance today, I head for the Lakes and give thanks for that.

The message from Helvellyn: *Find the contrast in your life. Don't get stale – try change. You might just love it.*

The island that made me understand how many worlds are right here on our doorstep: the Isle of Skye

When we talk about the British countryside, we often think of something idyllic, easy on the feet and knees, as well as on the eye – yet the Isle of Skye is fifty miles of stark volcanic magnificence. It's so remote you have to work hard to get there, but when you do cross from the mainland, either by road over the Skye Bridge or on the forty-five-minute ferry, you enter a very different world. Like the five international walks I've highlighted, the toughest treks on Skye are globally known destinations which draw serious, experienced walkers and climbers from around the world. (Do not attempt them unless this is you, or you are fit and ambitious and hire a professional guide to go with you.) I won't try to explain the island's history here; suffice to say, it's enough to get members of the Geological Society *very* excited. The most challenging mountains are those of the Black Cuillin range, the eroded magma chamber of a huge volcano, sculpted by glaciers and the weathering of the last sixty million years or so. There are boulder hills, steep scree slopes and knife-edge ridges, plus eleven Munros (Scottish mountains over 3,000 feet or 914 metres) in one seven-mile stretch. But the island also has many gentler, safer walks which will offer arresting views and a sense of freedom – and make you feel a very long way from home indeed.

The message from Skye: *Volcanoes mark the end of an old life and the beginning of a new one. They're disruptors – and the world needs them.*

The sea views responsible for redrawing my horizons: Cornwall, from Porthleven to Lizard Point

The artist's palette of colours Mother Nature used in Cornwall seems to come in shades marked 'extra vivid'. On a sunny day, the sea is Caribbean blue, the sands are golden and the clifftops are one hundred per cent chlorophyll. But they're not enough to make me take my eyes off the horizon, the most bewitching bit of a walk to Britain's southernmost tip. This route takes in perfect fishing villages and Halzephron Cove (Halzephron meaning 'Cliff of Hell' in Cornish because of a mythical freak wave that is said to come once every seven years) and even the old Marconi wireless station, from where the first transatlantic radio signals were sent across the water to Newfoundland in 1901. I love seeing it, because it reminds me of how much humans benefit from connection.

This walk also includes Kynance Cove, said by some to be the prettiest beach in Britain, with its sea stacks and white sands and clear water. So why is my favourite memory standing in the teeth of a gale on Lizard Point, where a gust of wind sneaked in between the lining and the outer of my coat, blowing it up like a balloon? Another notch on the Beaufort Scale, and I would have been airborne with the gulls. It's because this walk down the Lizard is all about big winds, open seas and distant horizons; it's a beckoning invitation to travel.

The message from the Lizard: *Even when you have to look down to keep your footing, don't forget to look out as well.*

The path that teaches you life isn't just one gorgeous bit after another: the Coast to Coast Walk

It would be impossible to walk 195 miles from one side of England to the other and have every step look stunning. That's why I'm including the Coast to Coast Walk from St Bees in Cumbria to Robin Hood's Bay in North Yorkshire. I love it, but some stretches can be . . . boring. Mostly, it's an exhilarating tramp through three national parks – the Lake District, the Yorkshire Dales and the North York Moors – but not every moment of the fourteen or so days it will take you are going to be box-office beautiful. The funny thing is that Alfred Wainwright created the Coast to Coast Walk because he hated the Pennine

Way, so I don't feel disloyal saying that one section of it (I won't say which one, because it might be different for you) just makes me want to put my head down and get through. Also, I think Wainwright hated much more of the Pennine Way! My point is that you start and end in beauty on the Coast to Coast, and you walk through a lot of magnificent scenery on the way, but there are some stretches where you have to grit your teeth and accept its imperfections – just like life.

The message from the Coast to Coast Walk: *Keep going*.

10

Walk Yourself Happy: Next Steps

'There is no real ending. It's just the
place where you stop the story.'
Frank Herbert, author[1]

Cancer saved my life.

That may seem a strange thing to say, but it opened my eyes to what was happening around me and what I was doing to myself.

In my life before diagnosis, everything I achieved was at breakneck speed. I wanted it all, and pushed myself emotionally and physically to reach impossible goals.

'Time is free, but it's priceless', as the saying goes.

And looking back, I didn't value it at all.

I shoved at the edges of it to manipulate hours and whole weeks to suit my agenda. With the momentum I built, I pushed my body to unnatural limits and forced it into unnatural rhythms. And I didn't recognise what I was doing, so I wasn't nourishing any other parts of me that might compensate or add some balance.

Until that ultrasound, when a pinprick of darkness upended my world – and any sense of my own agency in it.

'We have to let you go.'

'We're repossessing your house.'

'I'm leaving you.'

'Your partner, sister, brother, child, best friend, is dead.'

'You have cancer.'

These are probably the five most devastating life-changing things that we can be told. I've been on the receiving end of three of them. The impact of each was very different, but I can testify that there is nothing – nothing – like being diagnosed with a deadly illness to make you completely re-evaluate.

When I talked about Japan and the Nakasendō trail in the last chapter, I said I wasn't a religious person, but I do feel an affinity with Buddhist teachings. Here's one that has new meaning for me. When asked: 'What's the biggest mistake we make?' the Buddha's reply is: 'The biggest mistake is you think you have time . . .'

Well, that ultrasound exam was the moment I realised I might not have much time left at all. Tomorrow isn't guaranteed.

I have spoken to many experts in my research for *Walk Yourself Happy*. The science of time, the idea of it, that's Oliver Burkeman's speciality, and his words resonated with me.

He said we'll never have enough time to do everything, and learning how to let go of some of your hopes and apparent obligations is liberating. You have to relinquish some things to *make* time for others, and ultimately, it's the sacrifice that gives your choice meaning.

What the last couple of years have taught me is that since you are a finite person in a world with almost infinite choices and possibilities, you'd be wise to prioritise those choices that serve your health and make you happy while you are here.

It's what I have done, and it's what I will continue to do for the rest of my life. That was the unbreakable promise I made myself when I woke up from my mastectomy. I think it's a pretty universal response.

We all feel – occasionally – like throwing our deck of cards up in the air and seeing how they come down. Mostly we don't, because we can't. We have partners and children, or perhaps ageing parents to care for, a home to run and a living to earn.

Revolution isn't always possible, or right or kind. Evolution, that's natural.

Walk Yourself Happy is my manifesto for achievable and sustainable change – and thank you, by the way, for walking this far with me.

Now that you are here, reading this last chapter, I hope you're inspired to try some of the things in my book, and if you do, I hope they'll help you gain some space in your life, and let Mother Nature back in.

I have spoken about the pillars of human health: nutrition, sleep, exercise, breathwork and a peaceful mind. Re-examining your relationship with each of them will definitely 'cost' you time, but it may add longevity, and it'll certainly improve the quality of your life – so what do you have to lose?

Here are my top takeaways.

 ## The *Walk Yourself Happy* to-do list

- **Enjoy nature snacks** – Take regular breaks and get into nature, go into the garden, sniff the window box or watch the clouds. Do it for several minutes or more, and do it regularly throughout the day.
- **Get some morning light** – Between 7am and 9am, expose yourself to the magic morning light, setting off a hormone cascade in your body that prepares you for the rest of the day.
- **Sleep** – Take it seriously. This is when your body repairs and recharges. If you don't sleep well, all your bodily functions are affected. Remember – sleep deprivation is a form of torture.
- **Breathe** – There are so many breathwork practices to choose from. Find the one that works for you, and do it daily.
- **Exercise** – The data is clear: exercise delays actual death and helps prevent cognitive and physical decline more than any other single intervention. If it was a pill, you wouldn't believe it could have the impact it does.
- **Make time for good nutrition** – We live in a time of conspicuous abundance in the Western world; we are overfed and yet

> undernourished. Avoid processed food and cut out (or cut
> down) refined sugar. Feed your body goodness. And try
> taking a walk after every meal, or even running up and down
> the stairs for a few minutes; this reduces inflammatory glucose
> spikes and helps digestion.
> - **Find ways to manage stress** – Learn to meditate or practise
>   mindfulness or gratitude. Go solo: take the time every day to
>   be alone and to just *be*. Whatever that looks like for you.
> - **Walk. Every. Day.**

The last one on the list is, of course, the cornerstone of my
philosophy because you reap physical and mental benefits with
every step you take.

There is a growing body of science that suggests that 'sitting
still is the new smoking' – one day we'll look back on it and be
astonished it was ever normal. We are bipeds for a reason. I
know I said that in the introduction, but I'm saying it again here,
to remind you.

Sometimes, I walk with a brisk physical energy, to improve my
fitness; at other times, walking is one of the ways I meditate,
making a conscious effort to connect with the world around me,
and with myself.

In ancient Greek philosophy, *ataraxia* is a state of freedom
from emotional disturbance, a place of robust equanimity.
Walking can give you this. Being present is a lost skill, which
means I should probably add one more thing to that *Walk
Yourself Happy* to-do list above: try walking to more places
with your phone switched off. (I left mine at home when I did the
school run this morning. Imagine that – twenty-five minutes
without a phone!)

Actually, there's still one more rule to come, and it's a lovely
one: be sociable. Seek out your friends, family and neighbours
to create a community. There's an old proverb that says, 'If
you want to walk fast, walk alone, but if you want to walk far,

walk together.' So go and find someone to get your fix with occasionally.

Walking with friends and family is now my favourite way to spend time together. I've always had hiking buddies or film crews to go on outdoor adventures with, but recently I've been walking more with my friends (hello Anita, Kate, Naomi, Melissa, Inga, Sarah, David and Jayne – not you, Amanda, you're my gym bunny). We've stomped through parks and ambled around city streets enjoying in-depth conversations, helping each other navigate tricky times, laughing and even reading poetry aloud. The kind of things you'd more usually do over lunch or dinner, but somehow walks are easier to fit in. Shall we walk to work together? Shall we take a walk before the house is awake? See you at lunchtime?

Sometimes we walk side by side, other times one in front of the other, swapping places for no particular reason. The space between us gives our conversation time to breathe, with no need to fill the gaps. There's strength and motivation in our shared experience. If you're wondering where to start, sometimes being part of something 'more than one' helps. It's less daunting.

You might also bear in mind Theodore Roosevelt's brilliant advice: 'Do what you can, with what you have, where you are.' He always admitted borrowing it from someone else, but whatever its origin, it's a sound guiding principle. I guess it's the forerunner to Oliver Burkeman's suggestion that the difference between doing something for one or two or three minutes and not doing something at all is huge. But here is an important reminder to ourselves for those moments when we say, 'I don't have the time for that.' Exercising for sixty minutes a day is four per cent of your day; meditating for fifteen minutes is one per cent of your day.

So start by working out what you want and need and how to make way for these things in your life with what you've got available. It might be something as simple as switching off your phone, that little super-computer which has your brain permanently set to 'turbo', choosing instead to drench yourself in the morning light for ten minutes while thinking of three things which make you grateful. Maybe go cold turkey on the box sets for a while and discover what else you can do with that time.

If you don't make time for your health, you'll be forced to make time for your illness. That was me. It took cancer to make me make change.

Don't let it be you.

So let me finish by telling you how I made changes in my own life, which had ossified into busy-ness and a lack of care for myself. It was October 2021. I'd just had my mastectomy and was newly discharged from hospital.

The story begins in my back garden, a little pocket of nature that I love with all my heart. My partner and sister had helped me downstairs; I was wrapped in a blanket, unsteady on my feet and woozy with painkillers. But the pull of the green outside was strong, I could feel it through the big glass doors at the end of my kitchen.

Tentatively, I made my way through them into a glorious autumn day of crunchy leaves and scudding skies and mellow sun. I sank down on to my wooden bench and felt the full wattage of Mother Nature. I half-wondered if I'd conjured it, because I wanted and needed it so badly. There was light in my eyes, birdsong in my ears and sunshine on my face. Sitting at our garden table, which is a large fallen tree trunk propped up on steel legs, I admired the grain with my fingertips and the tough rigidity of the wood, a counterpoint to my weakness. I looked at my watch. The children would be coming home in half an hour, but for now I could just sit, enfolded.

That fragment of time outdoors held both an ending and a beginning for me. I hadn't conjured it; this was what hope felt like.

And I knew I had to go and give thanks on Mam Tor.

The mother of all hills

When you start young, walking gets into your bones. It feels like it's 'laced in our marrow, steeped in our blood' – thank you, Julia Baird, friend and author of *Phosphorescence* and *Bright Shining* (and a fellow cancer survivor) for that wonderful expression.

I have many special places that remind me of family and belonging and nature. I hope you do, too; and if you don't, I trust this will be the nudge you need to find some. Soon.

One of mine is Mam Tor in the Peak District, a place of beauty and serenity lovingly maintained for us all by the National Trust.

Mam Tor means Mother Hill, and it's part of the network of trails that helped me discover hiking with my dad when I was at secondary school. My mum and dad walked up it on their honeymoon a lifetime ago, and I've been back many times, sometimes for myself and sometimes for work, filming *Countryfile* or one of my walking shows.

It is meshed with our family life, and now it would be my place of pilgrimage.

It's only 517 metres high, but, for a pretty modest climb, you get one of the most iconic views in the country, staring over the Edale Valley to Kinder Scout, the tallest point in the Peaks.

My partner Gerry and our three children came with me; so did my parents (both in their mid-eighties) and my sister Gina. It was a first for us – I'd never been up Mam Tor with my mum, and it was the first hike my parents had ever done with their grandchildren. It was bittersweet, because I accepted, even while we were climbing, that we would never do it together again. (My dear friend and fellow presenter Matt Baker is a gifted artist and at the end of this chapter you can find a sketch he did of all of us on top of Mam Tor, his gift to me. We may not make it up mob-handed a second time but we will always have this precious memory preserved for ever, in ink, straight from Matt's imagination.)

Dad has wonky old knees now, swollen and sore from arthritis, so my heart burst when I saw my then ten-year-old son

Zeph take his forearm to gently encourage him up the path. 'Come on, Papou!' he sang.

I had my mum's hand clasped in mine, and we stopped to rest at rocks along the way.

'Is it much further?' she asked, with exactly the same ripple in her laughter that her own mother (YiYi) had had.

'The Greek gene is strong,' I thought to myself, feeling the happy ties of my family history stretching across four generations of women – from YiYi to Mama Mou, down through Gina and me and on to my twin girls Zena and Xanthe.

At the top, the sun was shining, the sky was the brightest blue, and paragliders were catching the thermals, their canopies an explosion of colour, like exotic birds. There were more paragliders in the sky than I had ever seen before or since. The eight of us took each other's hands and held them high in the air, like a band about to take a bow. We sounded a cry of achievement into the valley down below.

We'd made it.

I'd made it.

Tears escaped from my eyes, rolling down my cheeks, impossible to hide. It was the kind of crying that is both glad and sad at the same time. It wasn't just Mam Tor we'd climbed, but some kind of emotional mountain, cramponing our way up with courage and love.

'What's wrong, Mummy?' asked one of my girls.

What do you say to a seven-year-old?

'I'm just happy, darling,' I told her, remembering the day, shortly after diagnosis, when she'd wondered if it was still OK to cuddle me when I had cancer. How far we'd all come.

Climbing Mam Tor with the people I love most in the world was an article of faith in my future. I needed to do it not just to give thanks, but to overwrite the despair and desolation and terror that cancer had brought into my life.

As the paragliders twirled above our heads, other people up on the summit came to see us. They recognised me, but also

Mum and Dad from their various appearances on my TV shows across the years.

'Hello, Mama Mou,' they called. (In my travel series about the Greek islands, I took Mum back to our family island Chios and called her Mama Mou throughout the show.)

As for Dad's fart-i-choke soup and his embarrassing Dad comments made to millions on national TV, the less said about that the better.

People wanted to take pictures and to say hello, but mostly they wanted to tell me they'd seen my documentary *Julia Bradbury: Breast Cancer & Me*. Many of them asked if I was OK. As is so often the case now when I'm out, a woman quietly confided, 'I'm going through it, too. Thank you for sharing your story. Very brave.'

Honestly, I'm not brave. As I said when I began these closing thoughts, I think cancer saved my life. I got it and I *had* to make changes. This book explains how I did it, and I hope it might help you. Fundamentally, I wrote it because I believe we can all walk ourselves happy, taking small steps and then big strides, through the glad days of our lives.

See you in a park, along the city streets or on a hill soon. I'll be the one hugging a tree.

THE BRADBURYS 'ON TOR'

Further reading

The Well-Gardened Mind by Sue Stuart-Smith

Notes from a Nervous Planet and *Reasons to Stay Alive* by Matt Haig

The Diet Myth by Tim Spector

Primal Living in a Modern World and *Hungry Woman* by Pauline Cox

Life Time: The New Science of the Body Clock by Professor Russell Foster

Chasing the Sun by Linda Geddes

Why We Sleep by Matthew Walker

In Praise of Walking: The New Science of How We Walk and Why it's Good For Us by Shane O'Mara

Conscious Breathing by Anders Olsson

The Oxygen Advantage by Patrick McKeown

Tree Glee: How and Why Trees Make Us Feel Better by Cheryl Rickman

Breath by James Nestor

The Healing Pond by James Erith

The Metabolic Approach to Cancer by Dr Nasha Winters (with Jess Higgins Kelley)

Good Relations by Janet Reibstein

Pain-less by Anne Welsh

The Alchemist by Paul Coelho

Useful resources

The charity Mind has an excellent website (mind.org.uk) with resources and recommendations that can help with mental health problems.

The Every Mind Matters website (nhs.uk/every-mind-matters) is run by NHS England and offers a range of resources and support.

If you would like to speak to a therapist, these websites have lists of accredited therapists:
British Association for Counselling and Psychotherapy (BACP) – bacp.co.uk
British Psychoanalytic Council (BPC) – bpc.org.yk
British Association for Behavioural and Cognitive Psycho-therapies (BABCP) – babcp.com

For advice and information on foot health, visit the Healthy Step website (healthystep.co.uk).

To learn more about Hannah Beadle's work on Green Exercise, visit the Wildfitness website (wildfitness.com).

Acknowledgements

I am privileged and spoilt beyond words when it comes to love in my life: thank you, Mum and Dad, Chrissi and Michael, for showering me with care and affection, and for being inspirational cancer thrivers. I am convinced my sister Gina would jump under a bus for me, which of course I'd never want – but to know someone has your back with such certainty is beyond a gift. My circle of good friends, including my SA family, live up to their name and have moved in quiet waves to support me for the past two years, for which I am eternally thankful and indebted. My partner Gerry and children Zeph, Xanthe and Zena give me reason to live and to put into practice everything I write about in this book. The secret treasure that is N also helps make so much possible alongside the Irish clan. To my wing-woman, journalist and writer Sarah Oliver, our friendship has grown so much working on this project together. Synchronised walks, endless Zooms and some tears along the way. ('There is no real ending. It's just the place you stop the story.') We even had a call when I was up a tree – very on brand! I'd also like to say thank you to all my fans and everyone who has written to me or messaged me on social media with words of encouragement, kindness and love. I am truly grateful, and, as you know having read the book, gratitude is something I now practise daily.

I must say a huge thank you to my publishing agent, Global MD of YMU Literary, Amanda Harris, who has been nothing but effusive from the moment I spoke to her about the idea for this book. Her colleague Anna Dixon has been a remarkable support too, full of such sage advice for one so young (at the time of writing as they say!). Thank you to my publisher, Jillian Young; project manager, Jillian Stewart; our illustrator, Louise Turpin; and all at Piatkus and Little, Brown for showing such confidence in me and this project, and to my copyeditor, Tara O'Sullivan, for demonstrating great patience and offering such good advice. Nick and Hannah at YMU Management you help me through every day.

Thank you to all the wonderful contributors (particularly 'our resident' psychiatrist and psychotherapist Sue Stuart-Smith) who have shared themselves, their knowledge, science and expertise – it has helped make *Walk Yourself Happy* what I hope is an essential companion, with evidence and compelling stories to back up the advice: Robin Hanbury-Tenison, Professor Dacher Keltner, Louise Trewern, Oliver Burkeman, Maude Hurst, Angela Scanlon, Professor Tim Spector, Pauline Cox MSc, Professor Russell Foster, Tim Peake, Anders Olsson, Patrick McKeown, Professor Shane O'Mara, James Erith, Dr Nasha Winters, Professor Janet Reibsten, Mike Parry, Anne Welsh, Charlie Corbett, Helen Branthwaite PhD, Hannah Beadle and Dr Gabrielle Lyons.

Thanks to Carly and the team at JD Sports and Laura and the team at the National Trust (who take care of the treasures like Mam Tor, the Peaks and the Lake District for all of us) and to my camping family at The Camping and Caravanning Club. David Venni you're not just an amazing photographer, you're a great friend. Gayle Rinkoff and Alice Theobald – you're the Glam Squad everyone envies. I also have to mention my friend Heidi van Loggerenberg, who has taught me so much about personalised medicine and set me on a new course when she took me under her wing in the early days of my breast cancer diagnosis.

The idea for this book was germinating long before I heard those life-changing words, though. I wanted to write a book about coping with twenty-first-century living and the 24/7 lifestyle, using nature and walking as the tools. Getting cancer made me interrogate lifestyle issues through a different lens, but the advice in here is not for the sick – it is universal. We are the CEOs of our bodies and the authors of our life story. Just before finishing this book the indefatigable and unforgettable Tina Turner passed away. 'At every moment we always have a choice, even if it feels as if we don't. Sometimes the choice may simply be to think a more positive thought.' Her words are a great reminder to us all to think differently, even when we think that it isn't possible.

My last thanks goes to Mother Nature.

Notes

Chapter 1

1 Kessler, R., *et al.*, 'Lifetime prevalence and age-of-onset distributions of Dsm-IV disorders in the National Comorbidity Survey Replication', *Archives of General Psychiatry*, 62(6), 2005, pp. 593–602

2 Slee, A., *et al.*, 'Trends in generalized anxiety disorders and symptoms in primary care: UK population-based cohort study', *British Journal of Psychiatry*, 219(3), pp. 158–64

3 Chan, S. and Debono, M., 'Replication of cortisol circadian rhythm: new advances in hydrocortisone replacement therapy', *Therapeutic Advances in Endocrinology and Metabolism*, 1(3), 2010, pp. 129–138

4 The World Health Organization, 'Radiation: The known health effects of ultraviolet radiation', 2017, who.int

5 White, P. *et al.*, 'Spending at least 120 minutes a week in nature is associated with good health and wellbeing', *Scientific Reports*, 9, 2019

6 Bragg, R., *et al.*, 'Wellbeing benefits from natural environments rich in wildlife: A literature review for The Wildlife Trusts by the University of Essex', 2015

7 'Julia Bradbury on Emotionally Challenging Work', *One to One*, interview with Dr Rory Conn, BBC Radio 4, 17 January 2017

8 Haig, Matt, *Notes on a Nervous Planet* (p. 21), Canongate Books, Kindle edition.

Chapter 2

1 American psychologist Martin E. P. Seligman and Tracy A. Steen, University of Pennsylvania, Nansook Park University of Rhode Island

2 Peterson, C., 'Spending on doing promotes more moment-to-moment happiness than spending on having', *Journal of Experimental Social Psychology*, 2020 88:103971 DOI:10.1016/j.jesp.2020.103971

3 Burkeman, Oliver, *Four Thousand Weeks: Time and How to Use It*, Vintage, 2021

Chapter 3

1 Harvard Health Publishing, 'How much will fried foods harm your heart?', health.harvard.edu, 1 April 2021
2 Ganesan, K., Sukalingham, K., and Xu, B., 'Impact of consumption of repeatedly heating cooking oils on the incidence of various cancers – a critical review', *Critical Reviews in Food Science and Nutrition*, 59(3), pp. 488–505, 2019
3 Cloake, F., 'Are sausages bad for you?', *Guardian*, 7 March 2013
4 Ferdman, R., 'Where people eat the most sugar and fat', *Washington Post*, 5 February 2015
5 Sangor-Katz, M., 'You'd be surprised at how many foods contain added sugar', *New York Times*, 21 May 2016
6 https://www.cancerresearchuk.org/about-cancer/causes-of-cancer/body-weight-and-cancer/how-does-obesity-cause-cancer
7 Laing, B., and Crowley, J., 'Is undergraduate nursing education sufficient for patient's nutrition care in today's pandemics? Assessing the nutrition knowledge of nursing students: An integrative review', *Nurse Education in Practice*, 54, July 2021

Chapter 4

1 NIH Research Matters, 'How sleep clears the brain', National Institutes of Health, nih.gov, 28 October 2013
2 Staughton, J., 'Do we sleep better in cold or warm rooms?', Science ABC, scienceabc.com, 16 January 2022
3 Shoen, S., 'Biphasic sleep: What it is and how it works', Sleep Foundation, sleepfoundation.org, May 2023
4 Ananth, S., 'Sleep apps: current limitations and challenges', *Sleep Science*, 14(1), 2021, pp. 83–6
5 Sheehan, C., *et al.*, 'Are US adults reporting less sleep?: Findings from sleep duration trends in the National Health Interview Survey, 2004–2017', *Sleep*, 42(2), February 2019
6 IARC Monographs Vol 124 group, 'Carcinogenicity of night shift work', *Lancet Oncology*, 20(8), August 2019
7 'How the Intensity of Night Shift Work Affects Breast Cancer Risk', Int J Environ Res Public Health. 2021 May; 18(9): 4570. Published online 26 April 2021 doi: 10.3390/ijerph18094570PMCID: PMC8123502PMID: 33925799
8 Marshall, L., 'Can't get to sleep? A wilderness weekend can help', University of Colorado, Colorado.edu, 1 February 2017
9 Camping and Caravanning Club Research https://www.campingandcaravanningclub.co.uk/media-centre/surveys-and-reports/the-outjoyment-report/?

Chapter 5

1 Niazi, I. K., *et al.*, 'EEG signatures change during unilateral yogi nasal breathing', *Scientific Reports*, 12, 2022

2 Cromie, W. J., 'Meditation changes temperatures', *Harvard Gazette*, 18 April 2002

3 Quinn, D. 'What are dantian? The energy centers of Chinese medicine', healthline.com, 28 December 2020

4 Wikipedia, 'Pneuma', Wikipedia.org

Chapter 7

1 World Health Organization, 'Falls', who.int, 26 April 2021

2 Hillet, C. E., *et al.*, 'Prevalence and impact of chronic musculoskeletal disorders in the community', *Archives of Physical Medicine and Rehabilitation*, 93(10), 2012, pp. 1801–7

3 Hill, M., Branthwaite, H., and Chockalingham, N., 'The relationship between arch height and foot length: implications for size grading', *Applied Ergonomics*, 59, 2017, pp. 243–50

4 Chicharro-Luna, E., *et al.*, 'The influence of sock composition on the appearance of foot blisters in hikers', *Journal of Tissue Viability*, 31(2), May 2022, pp. 315–18

5 Tichet, J., *et al.*, 'Prevalence of sarcopenia in the French senior population', *Journal of Nutrition Health and Aging*, 12, pp. 202–6

6 Hébert-Losier, K. *et al.*, 'Updated reliability and normative values for the standing heel-rise test in healthy adults', *Physiotherapy*, 103(4), 2017, pp. 446–52

7 Araujo, C. G., *et al.*, 'Successful 10-second one-legged stance performance predicts survival in middle-aged and older individuals', *British Journal of Sports Medicine*, 56(17), 2022, pp. 975–80

8 Harvard Health Publishing, 'Improve your balance by walking', health. harvard.edu, 18 September 2022

Chapter 8

1 Sport England, 'Inactive people', sportengland.org

2 'Mini marathons: Tireless toddlers cover more than two and a half miles a day (but that includes 102 falls)', *Daily Mail*, 23 November 2012

3 University of Cambridge, 'Pedestrians choose healthy obstacles over boring pavements, study finds', cam.ac.uk, 5 December 2022

4 Anthony, A., 'The island of long life', *Guardian*, 31 May 2013

5 Spector, N. '"Blue Zones": 6 secrets to borrow from people who live the longest', nbcnews.com, 20 October 2018

6 University of Leicester, 'Stop the clocks: Brisk walking may slow biological ageing process, study shows', le.ac.uk, 20 April 2022

7 Konkel, L. 'Does the color green boost exercise's effects?', livescience.com, 30 May 2013

8 Klarlund Pedersen, B. 'Muscles and their myokines', *Journal of Experimental Biology*, 214(2), January 2011

9 Severinen, M.C.K. and Klarlund Pedersen, B. 'Muscle–organ crosstalk: the emerging roles of myokines', *Endocrine Reviews*, 41(4), August 2020, pp. 594–609

Chapter 10

1 Frank Herbert, California State College, Fullerton: Herbert was interviewed by Willis McNelly on the subject of his science fiction novels